BEGIN
ITAL

An Introduction to Conversational Italian

OTTAVIO NEGRO
and
JOSEPH HARVARD

With Illustrations by
PATRICIA ADAMSON

UNIVERSITY OF LONDON PRESS LTD

Tape recordings of *Beginners' Italian* are available from the Tutor-Tape Company Ltd, 258 Wimbledon Park Road, London SW19.

SBN 340 08574 6

First published 1961
Second edition

University of London Press Ltd
St Paul's House, Warwick Lane, London EC4

Filmset by Keyspools Ltd, Golborne, Lancs.
Printed in Great Britain by C. Tinling & Co Ltd, Liverpool, London and Prescot

PREFACE

This course is based on considerable practical experience in teaching beginners to speak Italian. It is essential for a student who wishes to learn the conversational language to study it from the very beginning; moreover, as the spoken language is the easiest form of the language, this approach is particularly suitable for all beginners, no matter what their ultimate purpose in learning the language may be.

The ability to speak a language cannot be gained from grammar study or reading, but like any other skill it can be acquired only through systematic and diligent practice. This book provides the material for such practice and presents it in the most suitable way for easy memorising and assimilation.

The lessons in the book have therefore been planned along the following lines. Each lesson begins with a short dialogue which should be thoroughly committed to memory. It will be seen that the great majority of the sentences learnt will serve as models for the formation of numerous other sentences, by the replacement of any word or word-group in the sentence with others of similar structure. This process of substitution is clearly shown in each lesson by the arrangement of several examples of sentence patterns in the form of 'substitution tables'. These combine several interchangeable word-groups and enable the student to form from them a large number of useful sentences. The student should read aloud as many combinations as possible by taking in turn one entry from each column in the table until all have been completely assimilated and each sentence can be immediately recalled.

This approach to the learning of a language does not exclude the treatment of grammar. However, grammar itself is not language: it is merely information about it, and when presented, as in this book, after the appearance and practice of each new language form it loses the unpleasant aura which it possesses for many students, and becomes a welcome clarification.

In the experience of the authors, fluency in any foreign language can be achieved only through practice comparable to—and as necessary as—the finger exercises which must be mastered when learning to play the piano. The method followed in this book ensures that correct expressions only are learnt, and enables the student to proceed confidently from the simple Italian in the present volume to the more complex forms of expression introduced in the subsequent volumes of the series. These are not merely sequels to *Beginners' Italian* but also companion books for use in conjunction with it. By its very nature, *Beginners' Italian* can give only a piecemeal introduction to Italian grammar, but the second book in the series, *Conversational Italian*, contains a systematic grammar of the spoken language, as well as a number of useful conversations concerned with foreign travel. Other features of the book are classified lists of the more important idioms for everyday conversation and a great number of sentence-building tables for further fluency practice.

The study of his textbooks will give a student a good basic knowledge of the rudiments of the language. As soon as possible, however, he should start reading some *real* Italian: i.e., texts written for the enjoyment of Italian people. In order to provide a selection of such material a companion book to this course, *Italian for Pleasure*, has been published. Many of the items selected are easy enough for a student to read during his first year of study.

A full explanation of the authors' method, and practical advice in the use of the course, are given in *Teaching Adults to Speak a Foreign Language*, which also serves as a Teachers' Book to the series.

In conclusion, the authors wish to thank Miss P. Adamson, of Camera Talks, for her charming illustrations and Mr. R. S. Kirkman, of the University of London Press Ltd, for his valuable assistance in the preparation of this course.

O. N.
J. H.

CONTENTS

PRONUNCIATION

Italian pronunciation follows definite rules which, once mastered, make it possible for almost every word to be pronounced correctly. The pronunciation indicated here is the recognised standard form as it is taught in Italian schools and understood all over the country. There are, however, considerable regional variations.

Vowels

Italian vowels are pure sounds. That is to say, the position of lips, tongue and jaws remains the same whilst the sound is uttered. This has to be constantly borne in mind when consulting the following table. The English equivalents given do not have quite the same sounds, as most English vowels are not pure sounds but diphthongs. For example, the *o* in h*o*me is pronounced as a mixture of two sounds, something like h*o*-*e*m. Such diphthongs do not exist in Italian. Even when vowels follow each other, each one must be distinctly and separately pronounced.

The difference between stressed and unstressed vowels is very slight and is shown mainly by the lengthening of the stressed vowel. Whereas in English unstressed vowels are often rendered with an obscure, neutral sound (as in the last syllables of *specimen* or *sofa*), in Italian both stressed and unstressed vowels retain their pure sound in all positions.

All vowels should be pronounced well forward in the mouth.

VOWEL	PRONUNCIATION	EXAMPLES
a	as in *father*[1]	la casa, *house*
e	as in *get*[2]	la neve, *snow*
i	as in *machine*	i nidi, *nests*
o	as in *hot*	il nonno, *grandfather*
u	as in *put*	tutto, *all*

[1] The pronunciation is shorter before two or more consonants, e.g. *canto, maschera.*

[2] Strictly speaking, both *e* and *o* have an open and a close sound, but this distinction is often ignored by even the most educated Italians. On the other hand *è* (= *is,* third person singular of *to be*), must be pronounced open, more like the letter *a* in *bad.*

Consonants

Double consonants have the same sound as single consonants but are pronounced with greater emphasis, as if one consonant were at the end of one word and the other at the beginning of the next.

Consonants are pronounced as in English, with the following exceptions:

CONSONANT	PRONUNCIATION	EXAMPLES
c	(1) before *a*, *o*, *u* and before consonants, as in *car*	il carro, *cart* credere, *to believe*
	(2) before *e* and *i*, as *ch* in *church*	la cera, *wax* la città, *town*
ch	as in *chemist*	l'occhio, *eye*
g	(1) before *a*, *o*, *u* and before consonants (except *l* and *n*), as in *good*	la gola, *throat* il grasso, *fat*
	(2) before *e* or *i*, as in *gin*	il ginocchio, *knee*
gh	as in *ghost*	il ghiaccio, *ice*
gli	similar to *lli* in *billiards*. (In the following words, however, *gli* is pronounced as in *angle*: *anglicano,* Anglican; *glicerina,* glycerine; *geroglifico,* hieroglyphic; *negligente,* negligent)	il figlio, *son*
gn	similar to *ni* in *onion*	il bagno, *bath*
h	is always silent. As we have seen above, it is added to *c* and *g* to harden their sounds in front of *e* and *i*	
qu	as in *quite*	quattro, *four*
r	is trilled by vibrating the tongue, in the Scottish manner	la sera, *evening* il ferro, *iron*

s	(1) as in *rose* between vowels, or when followed by the consonants *b*, *d*, *g*, *l*, *m*, *n*, *r*, *v*	la rosa, *rose* lo sbaglio, *mistake*
	(2) as in *sand* in all other cases, or when it is double	la seta, *silk* rosso, *red*
sc	like *sh* before *e* or *i*; otherwise like *sk*	la scelta, *choice* scuro, *dark*
z	has two sounds: it is sometimes soft (voiced), like the *ds* in *goods*, sometimes sharp (unvoiced), like the *ts* in *nuts*. There are no general rules, but for guidance bear in mind that *z* at the beginning of a word is usually voiced, and that double *z* is usually unvoiced.	la zia, *aunt* la forza, *strength* le nozze, *wedding*

Stress, Accent, Apostrophe

As a general rule, the stress in an Italian word of more than one syllable falls on the penultimate syllable.

The accent (which is usually grave) is used only when the stress occurs on the final vowel of a word. This vowel must then be sharply pronounced, as in *città*, town; *avrò*, I shall have.

The accent is also written on the words *già*, already; *giù*, down; *più*, more; *può*, he can; and on certain monosyllabic words in order to distinguish them from others of identical spelling but different meaning:

chè, *because*	che, *that*
là, *there*	la, *the* (f.)
nè, *nor*	ne, *of it, of them*
sè *himself, themselves*	se, *if*
sì, *yes*	si, *himself*
è, *is*	e, *and*
dà, *gives*	da, *from*

The apostrophe indicates that a vowel has been dropped (generally in order to obtain a smooth link between one word and the next), as in *l'amica* (instead of *la amica*).

In those exceptional cases where neither of the last two syllables is stressed, or where the correct stress is not readily apparent, the stressed vowel has been indicated in this book by printing it in different type, e.g. *libero* or l*i*bero.

Intonation

The way in which the voice rises and falls in connected speech cannot be learnt from a book. The best way to learn it is to hear it spoken and to try to imitate it. The broadcasts of Radio Italiana, on 366 and 457 metres, will help in the acquisition of the correct intonation.

Capital Letters

Initial capital letters are used for proper nouns, e.g.

Maria, Europa

Adjectives of nationality have small initial letters, unless they form part of a geographical designation, e.g.

un libro italiano	*an Italian book*
il Golfo Persiano	*the Persian Gulf*

Names of months, days and seasons have small initial letters, e.g.

una dom*e*nica di primavera	*a spring Sunday*
un giorno in aprile	*a day in April*

THE ALPHABET

LETTER	ITALIAN NAME	LETTER	ITALIAN NAME
a	*a*	n	*enne*
b	*bi*	o	*o*
c	*ci*	p	*pi*
d	*di*	q	*qu (pronounced koo)*
e	*e*	r	*erre*
f	*effe*	s	*esse*
g	*gi*	t	*ti*
h	*acca*	u	*u*
i	*i*	v	*vi*
l	*elle*	z	*zeta*
m	*emme*		

j, *k*, *w*, *x* and *y* are not used in Italian. When used to spell foreign words they are called *i lungo, cappa, doppio vi, ics, i greco.*

NUMERALS

CARDINAL

1 uno (un, una)	13 tr*e*dici
2 due	14 quatt*o*rdici
3 tre	15 qu*i*ndici
4 quattro	16 s*e*dici
5 cinque	17 diciass*e*tte
6 sei	18 diciotto
7 sette	19 diciannove
8 otto	20 venti
9 nove	21 ventuno
10 dieci	22 ventidue
11 *u*ndici	23 ventitrè
12 d*o*dici	30 trenta

Cardinal (*cont.*)

31 trentuno
32 trentadue
40 quaranta
50 cinquanta
60 sessanta
70 settanta
80 ottanta
90 novanta
99 novantanove
100 cento

101 centouno
110 centodieci
200 duecento
300 trecento
1.000 mille
1.500 millecinquecento
2.000 duemila
10.000 diecimila
100.000 centomila
1.000.000 un milione

Ordinal

1st il primo, la prima
2nd il secondo, la seconda
3rd terzo, –a
4th quarto, –a
5th quinto, –a
6th sesto, –a
7th s*e*ttimo, –a
8th ottavo, –a
9th nono, –a
10th d*e*cimo, –a
11th undic*e*simo, –a
12th dodic*e*simo, –a
13th tredic*e*simo, –a

14th quattordic*e*simo, –a
15th quindic*e*simo, –a
16th sedic*e*simo, –a
17th diciassett*e*simo, –a
18th diciott*e*simo, –a
19th diciannov*e*simo, –a
20th vent*e*simo, –a
21st ventun*e*simo, –a
22nd ventidu*e*simo, –a
23rd ventitre*e*simo, –a
100th cent*e*simo, –a
1,000th mill*e*simo, –a

Fractions

$\frac{1}{2}$ una metà
$\frac{1}{3}$ un terzo
$\frac{1}{4}$ un quarto
$\frac{1}{5}$ un quinto; *etc.*

$\frac{3}{4}$ tre quarti
$\frac{7}{8}$ sette ottavi
$3\frac{1}{2}$ tre e mezzo

Mezzo is the adjective corresponding to *la metà*; it agrees with the noun: *mezzo limone, mezza banana.*

Prima Lezione

Entri!

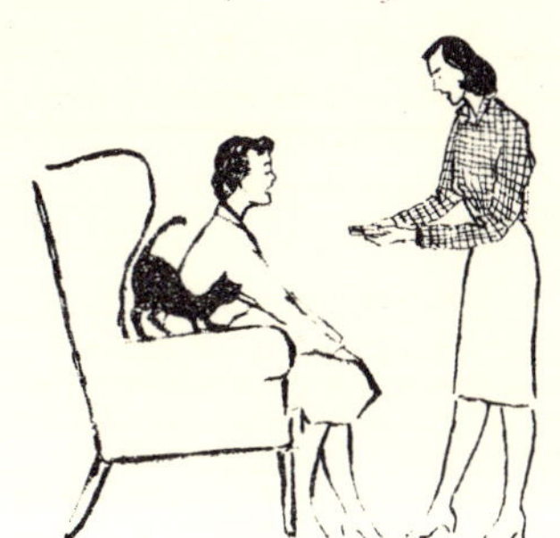

Fuma (lei)?

(Io) non fumo.

Non fumi!

Qui Si Parla Italiano

A: *Un signore.* B: *Una signora.*

A: Buongiorno,[1] signora[2] (signorina[3]).

B: Buongiorno, signore.[4]

[1] buongiorno, *good day (also used for good morning and good afternoon)*
[2] signora, *madam.*
[3] signorina, *miss.*
[4] signore, *sir.*

A: Entri,* prego![5]

B: (Lei) parla[6] italiano, vero?[7]

A: Un poco.[8] Non parla[9] inglese[10] (lei)?

B: (Io) non parlo[11] molto[12] bene.[13]

A: Fuma (lei)?* Prenda[14] una sigaretta.

B: Grazie![15]

A: Prego.[16]

* Items marked thus are explained through illustrations.

[5] prego, *please (see Explanation* 5).
[6] (lei) parla, *you speak*; lei *may be omitted* (*see Explanation* 1).
[7] vero, *don't you?* (*see Explanation* 6).
[8] un poco, *a little*.
[9] Non parla (lei)? *Don't you speak?*
[10] inglese, *English*.
[11] (io) non parlo, *I do not speak*.
[12] molto, *very*.
[13] bene, *well*.
[14] prenda, *take*.
[15] grazie, *thank you*.
[16] prego, *don't mention it* (*see Explanation* 5).

Fluency Practice

1. Entri! — *Come* (or *go*) *in!*
   Legga! — *Read!*
   Scriva! — *Write!*
   Guardi! — *Look!*
   Ascolti! — *Listen!*
   Ripeta! — *Repeat!*
   Parli italiano! — *Speak Italian!*

2. Non | entri! / guardi! / ascolti! / legga! / parli così in fretta! — *Don't* | *come* (or *go*) *in!* / *look!* / *listen!* / *read!* / *speak so fast!*

Non	entri!		*Don't*	*come* (or *go*) *in!*	
	guardi!			*look!*	
	ascolti!			*listen!*	
	legga!			*read!*	
	parli così in fretta!			*speak so fast!*	

3.

(Lei)	entra,	non è vero?	*You are*	*coming (going) in,*	*aren't you?*
	guarda,			*looking,*	
	ascolta,			*listening,*	
	legge,			*reading,*	
	parla,			*speaking,*	

4.

Entra (lei)?	*Are you*	*coming (going) in?*
Guarda (lei)?		*looking?*
Ascolta (lei)?		*listening?*
Legge (lei)?		*reading?*
Parla (lei)?		*speaking?*

5.	Non	entra (lei)? guarda (lei)? ascolta (lei)? legge (lei)? parla (lei)?	*Aren't you*	*coming (going) in?* *looking?* *listening?* *reading?* *speaking?*
6.	Sì, (io) No, (io) non	entro. guardo. ascolto. leggo. parlo.	*Yes, I am* *No, I am not*	*coming (going) in.* *looking.* *listening.* *reading.* *speaking.*

Explanations

1. As the endings of Italian verbs indicate person and number, the subject pronoun is omitted unless needed for clarity or emphasis.

2. No distinction is made in Italian between 'I speak' and 'I am speaking'. Both forms are expressed by *(io) parlo.*

3. The verb 'to do', as used to ask questions in English, is not expressed in Italian. In Italian a statement can be turned into a question merely by the intonation of the voice, or else the subject, when used, is placed after the verb or at the very end of the sentence, e.g.

(Lei) parla inglese o italiano?
Parla (lei) inglese o italiano? } *Do you speak English or Italian?*
Parla inglese o italiano (lei)?

4. A verb is made negative by placing *non* before it.

5. As a rule, Italians reply to thanks or apologies with *prego* ('don't mention it'). But *prego* means 'please' when used with a command or request, e.g.

Legga, prego. *Read, please.*

6. *vero?* or *non è vero?* (lit. true, isn't it true) corresponds to 'do you, don't you, is it, aren't you?' etc.

Seconda Lezione

Un signore entra.

Egli fuma una sigaretta.

Una signora sale le scale.

Essa canta.

Al Bar

A: *Un Americano.* B: *Un Inglese.* C: *Un Italiano.*

A: Fuma, signore?

B: No grazie, non fumo.

A: E[1] lei, signore?

C: Volentieri.[2] (Lei) è[3] molto gentile.[4] È[5] una sigaretta inglese, vero?

[1] e, *and.*
[2] volentieri, *gladly.*
[3] (lei) è, *you are.*
[4] gentile, *kind.*
[5] è, *it is.*

A: No, signore. È una sigaretta americana.[6]

C: È americano lei?

A: Sì,[7] sono[8] americano.

C: E lei, signore, è anche[9] lei americano?

B: No, io non sono americano. Io sono inglese. Ma[10] mia moglie[11] non è inglese; essa[12] è scozzese.[13]

C: Essa allora[14] parla inglese con[15] l'accento scozzese?

B: Proprio così.[16] Essa parla anche l'italiano con l'accento scozzese.

[6] *see Explanation* 4.
[7] sì, *yes*.
[8] sono, *I am*.
[9] anche, *also*
[10] ma, *but*.
[11] mia moglie, *my wife*.
[12] essa, *she*.
[13] scozzese, *Scottish*.
[14] allora, *then*.
[15] con, *with*.
[16] proprio così, *that is so*.

Fluency Practice

1.

Un signore	entra.	*A gentleman*	*is coming (going) in.*
Una signora	sale.	*A lady*	*is coming (going) up.*
Una signorina	parla.	*A young lady*	*is speaking.*
Un giovanotto	canta.	*A young man*	*is singing.*
Una ragazza	legge.	*A girl*	*is reading.*
Un ragazzo	scrive.	*A boy*	*is writing.*
Un uomo	guarda.	*A man*	*is looking.*
Una donna	ascolta.	*A woman*	*is listening.*
Uno studente	ripete.	*A student*	*is repeating.*

2.

È (egli)	un insegnante*	*Is he*	*a teacher* (m.)
È (essa)[1]	un'insegnante	*Is she*	*a teacher* (f.)
Non è (egli)	uno studente	*Is he not*	*a student* (m.)
Non è (essa)	una studentessa	*Is she not*	*a student* (f.)
Sì, (egli) è	un agente	*Yes, he is*	*a policeman*
Sì, (essa) è	una cameriera	*Yes, she is*	*a chambermaid*
No, (egli) non è	un cameriere	*No, he is not*	*a waiter*
No, (essa) non è	un'infermiera	*No, she is not*	*a nurse*
	un doganiere		*a customs official*

[1] In some parts of Italy *ella* is used instead of *essa*.

* In sentence-building tables which contain both statements and questions, punctuation has been omitted.

3.

Il signore	entra.	*The gentleman*	*is coming (going) in.*
La signora	non entra.	*The lady*	*is not coming (going) in.*
La signorina	sale.	*The young lady*	*is coming (going) up.*
L'insegnante	non sale.	*The teacher*	*is not coming (going) up.*
Lo studente	ascolta.	*The student*	*is listening.*
Il cameriere	non ascolta.	*The waiter*	*is not listening.*
Egli	parla.	*He*	*is speaking.*
Essa	non parla.	*She*	*is not speaking.*

4.

Parla	il signore?	*Is*	*the gentleman*	*speaking?*
Canta	la signora?		*the lady*	*singing?*
Suona	il ragazzo?		*the boy*	*playing? (an instrument)*
Danza	la ragazza?		*the girl*	*dancing?*

5.

Sì, (egli)	parla.	*Yes, he*	*is speaking.*
Sì, (essa)	canta.	*Yes, she*	*is singing.*
No, (egli)	non suona.	*No, he*	*is not playing.*
No, (essa)	non danza.	*No, she*	*is not dancing.*

6.

(Egli)	parla	poco.	*He*	*speaks*	*little.*
(Essa)	danza	un poco.	*She*	*dances*	*a little.*
	canta	molto.		*sings*	*much.*
	lavora	troppo.		*works*	*too much.*
	legge	molto poco.		*reads*	*very little.*
	scrive	bene.		*writes*	*well.*
		molto bene.			*very well.*
		abbastanza bene.			*fairly well.*
		male.			*badly.*

7.

(Io) sono	italiano[1] (italiana).	*I am*	*Italian.*
(Lei) è	inglese (inglese).	*You are*	*English.*
(Egli) è	scozzese (scozzese).	*He is*	*Scottish.*
(Essa) è	irlandese (irlandese).	*She is*	*Irish.*
	canadese (canadese).		*Canadian.*
	americano (americana).		*American.*
	francese (francese).		*French.*
	spagnolo (spagnola).		*Spanish.*
	tedesco (tedesca).		*German.*
	australiano (australiana).		*Australian.*

8.

Sono (io)	italiano?	*Am I*	*Italian?*
È (lei)	inglese?	*Are you*	*English?*
È (egli)	scozzese?	*Is he*	*Scottish?*
È (essa)	irlandese? etc.	*Is she*	*Irish? etc.*

[1] The adjectives of nationality usually begin with a small letter.

1. *Un* = a (an), before a masculine singular noun.
Uno = a (an), before a masculine singular noun beginning with *s* impure[1] or *z*.
Una = a (an), before a feminine singular noun. *Una* is reduced to *un'* before a noun beginning with a vowel.
2. *Il* = the, before a masculine singular noun beginning with a consonant.
Lo = the, before a masculine singular noun beginning with *s* impure[1] or *z*.
La = the, before a feminine singular noun beginning with a consonant.
L' = the, before a masculine or feminine noun beginning with a vowel.

3. In Italian all nouns (whether names of persons, animals or things) are either masculine or feminine. This distinction of gender is purely grammatical and does not necessarily imply that something is 'male' or 'female'.

Nouns ending in *–o* are generally masculine, and those ending in *–a* are generally feminine.[2]

There are exceptions to this rule, the most common of which are *la mano*, the hand (*f.*), and *la radio*, the radio (*f.*).

4. In Italian the adjective must agree in gender (and in number, as we shall see) with the noun it qualifies. Therefore an adjective ending in *–o* changes this into an *–a* when qualifying a feminine noun:

rosso, *red* (m.)→ rossa, *red* (f.)

Adjectives not ending in *–o* do not vary in the feminine:

verde, *green* (m. *or* f.)

5. Adjectives usually follow the noun, but certain short common adjectives like *bello* (beautiful), *buono* (good), *grande* (large) precede it.

[1] i.e., *s* followed by a consonant.

[2] Nouns ending in *–ione* and *–ù* are also feminine, but the latter are somewhat rare.

Terza Lezione

LA C*A*MERA

ALL'ALBERGO

A: *Il portiere dell'albergo.*[1] B: *Un signore.*

B: C'è una c*a*mera* l*i*bera?[2]

A: Abbiamo una c*a*mera p*i*ccola con bagno.[3]

B: Qual'[4]è il prezzo?[5]

A: Mille lire al giorno,[6] più il dieci per cento di serv*i*zio. Vuol[7] vedere[8] la c*a*mera?

B: Volentieri.[9]

1 il portiere dell'albergo, *reception clerk.*
2 l*i*bero, –a, *free.*
3 il bagno, *bath.*
4 qual' (= quale), *what, which.*
5 il prezzo, *price.*
6 al giorno, *per day.*
7 vuol (=vuole), *do you wish to.*
8 vedere, *to see.*
9 volentieri, *gladly.*

A: Vuol seguirmi,[10] signore? Prendiamo[11] l'ascensore.[12]

B: A che piano?[13]

A: Al secondo,[14] signore. Ecco[15] la *ca*mera. Le piace?[16]

B: È molto p*i*ccola. Non ha una *ca*mera più grande?[17]

A: No, signore. Per il momento no.

B: Va bene.

A: Ha un letto* grande e c*o*modo, una t*a*vola,* un guardaroba* e un cassettone.* C'è anche il tel*e*fono.

B: Dov'è[18] il bagno?

A: Qui a fianco.[19] Il rubinetto[20] dell'acqua[21] calda[22] è a destra[23] e il rubinetto dell'acqua fredda[24] a sinistra.[25]

[10] seguire, *to follow.*
[11] prendiamo, *let us take.*
[12] un ascensore, *lift.*
[13] il piano, *floor.*
[14] secondo, *second.*
[15] ecco, *here is.*
[16] le piace? *do you like it?*
[17] più grande, *larger.*
[18] dov'è, *where is.*
[19] a fianco, *by the side, next door.*
[20] il rubinetto, *tap.*
[21] l'acqua, *water* (f.).
[22] caldo, –a, *warm.*
[23] a destra, *on the right.*
[24] freddo, –a, *cold.*
[25] a sinistra, *on the left.*

Fluency Practice

1.

È	il	letto.	*It is*	*the*	*bed.*
Non è	un	bagno.	*It is not*	*a*	*bath.*
Questo è		tel*e*fono.	*This is*		*telephone.*
Questo non è		rubinetto.	*This is not*		*tap.*
Quello è			*That is*		
Quello non è	l'	albergo.	*That is not*		*hotel.*
	un	ascensore.			*lift.*

2.

È	la	sedia.	*It is*	*the*	*chair.*
Non è	una	t*a*vola.	*It is not*	*a*	*table.*
Questa è		*ca*mera.	*This is*		*room.*
Questa non è			*This is not*		
Quella è	l'	autom*o*bile.	*That is*		*car.*
Quella non è	un'	oliva.	*That is not*	*an*	*olive.*

3.

Sono	i	letti.	*They are*	*the*	*beds.*
Non sono		rubinetti.	*They are not*		*taps.*
Questi sono			*These are*		
Questi non sono	gli	alberghi.	*These are not*		*hotels.*
Quelli sono		ascensori.	*Those are*		*lifts.*
Quelli non sono		armadi.	*Those are not*		*cupboards.*

4.

Sono	le	s*e*die.	*They are*	*the*	*chairs.*
Non sono		t*a*vole.	*They are not*		*tables.*
Queste sono		c*a*mere.	*These are*		*rooms.*
Queste non sono		autom*o*bili.	*These are not*		*cars.*
Quelle sono		olive.	*Those are*		*olives.*
Quelle non sono		poltrone.	*Those are not*		*armchairs.*

5.

Il	letto	è	grande.	*The*	*bed*	*is*	*large.*
Questo	bagno	non è	p*i*ccolo.	*This*	*bath*	*is not*	*small.*
Quel	rubinetto			*That*	*tap*		
L'	albergo			*The*	*hotel*		
Quest'	ascensore			*This*	*lift*		
Quell'	arm*a*dio			*That*	*cupboard*		
ESSO				**IT** (*m.*)			

6.

La	s*e*dia	è	grande.	*The*	*chair*	*is*	*large.*
Questa	t*a*vola	non è	p*i*ccola.	*This*	*table*	*is not*	*small.*
Quella	c*a*mera			*That*	*room*		
L'	autom*o*bile			*The*	*car*		
Quest'	oliva			*This*	*olive*		
Quell'	*a*nitra			*That*	*duck*		
ESSA				**IT** (*f.*)			

7.

I	letti	sono	grandi.	*The*	*beds*	*are*	*large.*
Questi	rubinetti	non sono	p*i*ccoli.	*These*	*taps*	*are not*	*small.*
Quei	piatti			*Those*	*plates*		
Gli	alberghi			*The*	*hotels*		
Questi	ascensori			*These*	*lifts*		
Quegli	armadi			*Those*	*cupboards*		
ESSI				**THEY** (*m.*)			

8.

Le	s*e*die	sono	grandi.	*The*	*chairs*	*are*	*large.*
Queste	t*a*vole	non sono	p*i*ccole.	*These*	*tables*	*are not*	*small.*
Quelle	autom*o*bili			*Those*	*cars*		
	olive				*olives*		
ESSE				**THEY** (*f.*)			

9.

(Io) ho	una	grande c*a*mera.	*I have*	*a*	*large room.*
(Io) non ho		buona s*e*dia.	*I haven't*		*good chair.*
(Lei) ha		c*o*moda poltrona.	*You have*		*comfortable armchair.*
(Lei) non ha	un	grande letto.	*You haven't*		*large bed.*
(Egli) ha		buon albergo.	*He has*		*good hotel.*
(Essa) non ha		bagno nuovo.	*She hasn't*		*new bath.*

È	una	buona c*a*mera?	*Is it*	*a*	*good room?*
Non è		p*i*ccola val*i*gia?	*Isn't it*		*small suitcase?*
Ha (lei)			*Have you*		
Non ha (lei)	un	buon letto?	*Haven't you*		*good bed?*
Ha (egli)		grande albergo?	*Has he*		*large hotel?*
Non ha (egli)			*Hasn't he*		
Ha (essa)			*Has she*		
Non ha (essa)			*Hasn't she*		

11.	(Noi)	fumiamo.	*We*	*are smoking.*
		entriamo.		*are going*[1] *in.*
		saliamo.		*are going*[1] *up.*
		mangiamo.		*are eating.*

12.	Fumiamo.	*Let us*	*smoke.*
	Mangiamo.		*eat.*
	Entriamo.		*go in.*
	Saliamo.		*go up.*

[1] or *coming*.

Explanations

1. The plural of *il* is *i*, and the plural of *lo* and of *l'* masculine is *gli*.

The plural of *la* and of *l'* feminine is *le*.

2. Adjectives agree in gender and number with the nouns they qualify.

Adjectives ending in *–o* change this letter in the feminine into *–a*.

Those ending in *–e* and *–u* do not change.

3. Both nouns and adjectives change their final vowel into *–i* in the plural, except feminines in *–a* which change into *–e*. The few nouns and adjectives ending in *–u* do not change in the plural.

4. *Esso* = it, when replacing a masculine noun.

Essa = it, when replacing a feminine noun.

Essi = they, when replacing masculine plural nouns.

Esse = they, when replacing feminine plural nouns.

5. In connection with *noi* (=we), verbs end in *–iamo*. The same form of the verb expresses the imperative 'let us . . .'.

6. The final vowel of a word is dropped whenever a smoother passage to the next word results, provided that the clearness of meaning is retained. Therefore, as in this lesson's conversation passage, Italians prefer to say *vuol vedere* instead of *vuole vedere* (and certainly always *un buon letto* instead of *un buono letto*, as the ending of *buono* resembles the indefinite article).

7. *Quello*, in front of a noun, changes its ending in the same way as the definite article:

que*l* bagno, quel*lo* studente, quel*l'*ombrello,
que*gli* studenti, que*i* libri,
quel*la* matita, quel*l'a*nitra, quel*le* matite.

The adjective *bello* undergoes the same changes.

8. 'I like it', 'I like them', etc., take the form of 'it pleases me', 'they please me', etc., in Italian:

Le piace?	*Do you like it?*
Le pi*a*cciono?	*Do you like them?*
Mi piace; non mi piace.	*I like it; I don't like it.*
Mi pi*a*cciono; non mi pi*a*cciono.	*I like them; I don't like them.*
Le piace questo profumo?	*Do you like this perfume?*
No, non mi piace.	*No, I don't like it.*
Le pi*a*cciono le arance?	*Do you like oranges?*
Sì, mi pi*a*cciono.	*Yes, I like them.*
Non mi piace suo cugino.	*I don't like your cousin.*

Quarta Lezione

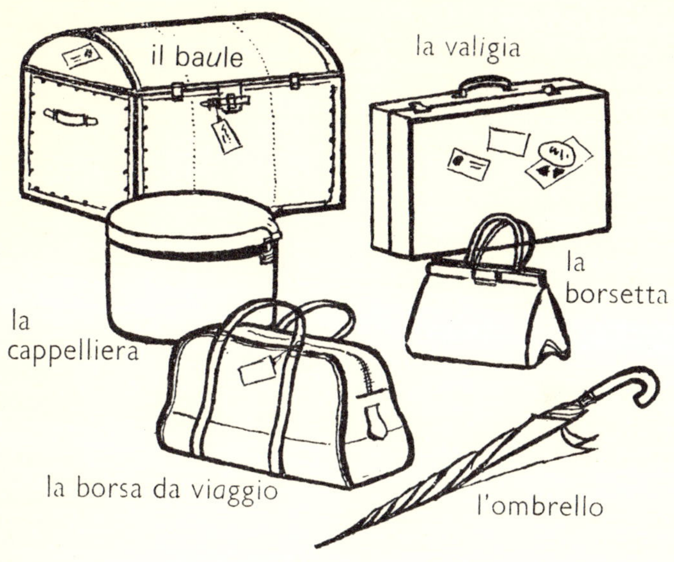

I BAGAGLI

I Bagagli

A: *Un signore.* B: *Un facchino.*[1]

A (*al telefono*): Faccia portare sù[2] i miei bagagli,* per favore.

(*Due minuti*[3] *più tardi*[4] *bussano*[5] *alla porta della camera N⁰* 18.[6])

A: Avanti!

B: Ecco i suoi bagagli, signore. Un baule,* due valige* e una borsa da viaggio.* Per primo[7] ecco il baule.

A: Lo metta su quella sedia davanti[8] alla finestra.

[1] il facchino, *porter.*
[2] faccia portare sù, *have brought up, send up.*
[3] il minuto, *minute.*
[4] più tardi, *later.*
[5] bussano, *someone knocks; there is a knock.*
[6] numero diciotto.
[7] per primo, *first.*
[8] davanti, *in front.*

B: Dove metto le valige?
A: Le metta dietro[9] al guardaroba.
B: E la borsa da vi*a*ggio?
A: La dia[10] a me. (*La posa*[11] *sulla tavola.*)
B: Questo è tutto,[12] signore.
A: Prenda,[13] questo è per[14] lei. (*Gli*[15] *dà*[16] *la mancia.*[17])
B: Molte gr*a*zie, signore.

[9] dietro, *behind.*
[10] la dia, *give it.*
[11] la posa, (*he*) *puts it.*
[12] tutto, *all.*
[13] prenda, *there you are* (*lit.* '*take*').
[14] per, *for.*
[15] gli, (*to*) *him.*
[16] dà, *gives.*
[17] la m*a*ncia, *tip.*

Fluency Practice

1. I vestiti sono	sul tavolino.	*The clothes are*	*on the small table.*
I vestiti non sono	nel ba*u*le.	*The clothes are not*	*in the trunk.*
Metta tutto	nel guardaroba.	*Put everything*	*in the wardrobe.*
Metta le cose	sulla t*a*vola.	*Put the things*	*on the table.*
Lo metta	nella vali*g*ia.	*Put it* (m.)	*in the suitcase.*
Non lo metta	nell'entrata.	*Don't put it*	*in the hall.*
La metta	di fianco al ba*u*le.	*Put it* (f.)	*beside the trunk.*
Non la metta	vicino all'arm*a*dio.	*Don't put it*	*near the cupboard.*
Li metta	davanti alla finestra.	*Put them* (m.)	*in front of the window.*
Non li metta	dietro alla t*a*vola.	*Don't put them*	*behind the table.*
Le metta	di fianco alla vali*g*ia.	*Put them* (f.)	*beside the suitcase.*
Non le metta	vicino alla porta.	*Don't put them*	*near the door.*

2. (Io) sono		qui.	*I am*		*here.*
(Tu) sei		là.	*You* (fam.) *are*		*there.*
(Lei)	è	nel giardino.	*You are*		*in the garden.*
(Egli)		sul tetto.	*He*	*is*	*on the roof.*
(Essa)		sull'*a*lbero.	*She*		*on the tree.*
(Esso)		davanti alla casa.	*It* (m.)		*in front of the house.*
(Essa)		dietro all'autorimessa.	*It* (f.)		*behind the garage.*
		di fianco alla scuola.			*beside the school.*
(Noi) siamo		vicino alla chiesa.	*We*	*are*	*near the church.*
(Voi) siete		lontano dalla stazione.	*You* (sing.)		*far from the station.*
(Loro)	sono		*You* (pl.)		
(Essi)			*They* (m.)		
(Esse)			*They* (f.)		

3. Prenda	il libro.	*Take*	*the book.*
Ecco	l'ombrello.	*Here is* (*are*)	*the umbrella.*
Porti	i vestiti.	*Bring*	*the clothes.*
	la vali*g*ia.		*the suitcase.*
	le cose.		*the things.*
	gli altri libri.		*the other books.*

4.	Lo	metta	nel cassetto.	*Put*	*it* (m.)	*in the drawer.*
	La		nell'arm*a*dio.		*it* (f.)	*in the cupboard.*
	Li		nella val*i*gia.		*them* (m.)	*in the suitcase.*
	Le		sulla t*a*vola.		*them* (f.)	*on the table.*

5.	(Io)	lo	prendo.	*I*	*take*	*it* (m.).
		la	guardo.		*look at*	*it* (f.).
		li	apro.		*open*	*them* (m.).
		le	chiudo.		*shut*	*them* (f.).

6.	(Egli)	lo	prende.	*He*	*takes*	*it* (m.).
	(Essa)	la	guarda.	*She*	*looks at*	*it* (f.).
		li	apre.		*opens*	*them* (m.).
		le	chiude.		*shuts*	*them* (f.).

7.	(Io) non		lo	tocco.	*I don't*		*touch*	*it* (m.).
			la	guardo.			*look at*	*it* (f.).
			li	tengo.			*keep*	*them* (m.).
			le	chiudo.			*shut*	*them* (f.).
	(Egli)	non	lo	tocca.	*He*	*doesn't*	*touch*	*it* (m.).
	(Essa)		la	guarda.	*She*		*look at*	*it* (f.).
			li	tiene.			*keep*	*them* (m.).
			le	chiude.			*shut*	*them* (f.).

8.	Lei	lo	prende?	*Do you*	*take*	*it* (m.)*?*
	Lei non	la	tiene?	*Don't you*	*keep*	*it* (f.)*?*
		li	guarda?		*look at*	*them* (m.)*?*
		le	chiude?		*shut*	*them* (f.)*?*

9.	Non	lo	prenda!	*Don't*	*take*	*it* (m.)*!*
		la	tocchi!		*touch*	*it* (f.)*!*
		li	chiuda!		*shut*	*them* (m.)*!*
		le	apra!		*open*	*them* (f.)*!*
	Non	lo	guardi!	*Don't*	*look at*	*him* (or it)*!*
		la				*her* (or *it*)*!*
		li				*them* (m.)*!*
		le				*them* (f.)*!*

10.	(Io) prendo	questo libro.	*I take*	*this book.*
	(Io) non prendo	questa matita.	*I don't take*	*this pencil.*
	(Io) preferisco	quel libro.	*I prefer*	*that book.*
	(Lei) prende	questi libri?	*Do you take*	*these books?*
	(Lei) non prende	queste matite?	*Don't you take*	*these pencils?*
	Lei preferisce	quei libri?	*Do you prefer*	*those books?*

Explanations

1. *The Definite Article ('the')*

	MASCULINE		FEMININE
SINGULAR	il	lo (l')	la (l')
PLURAL	i	gli (gl')	le

il is used before a		masculine singular noun beginning with consonant.
lo	,, ,,	masculine singular noun beginning with *s* impure[1] or *z*.
l'	,, ,,	masculine singular noun beginning with vowel.
la	,, ,,	feminine singular noun beginning with consonant.
l'	,, ,,	feminine singular noun beginning with vowel.
i	,, ,,	masculine plural noun beginning with consonant.
gli	,, ,,	masculine plural noun beginning with *s* impure,[1] *z, a, e, o, u.*
gl'	,, ,,	masculine plural noun beginning with *i*.
le	,, ,,	feminine plural noun.

2. The prepositions *a, di, da, in, su,* when followed by the definite article, are joined to it and form the following combinations:[2]

	A	DI	DA	IN	SU
joined to il:	al (*to the*)	del (*of the*)	dal (*from the*)	nel (*in the*)	*sul* (*on the*)
,, *lo:*	allo	dello	dallo	nello	sullo
,, *l':*	all'	dell'	dall'	nell'	sull'
,, *la:*	alla	della	dalla	nella	sulla
,, *i:*	ai	dei	dai	nei	sui
,, *gli:*	agli	degli	dagli	negli	sugli
,, *gl':*	agl'	degl'	dagl'	negl'	sugl'
,, *le:*	alle	delle	dalle	nelle	sulle

3. *The Indefinite Article* ('*a, an*')

un is used before a		masculine noun beginning with consonant.
uno	,, ,,	masculine noun beginning with *s* impure[1] or *z*.
una	,, ,,	feminine noun beginning with consonant.
un'	,, ,,	feminine noun beginning with vowel.

4. The pronouns *lo, la, li, le* are used in connection with verbs (and must not be confused with the articles *il, lo, la, i, gli, le,* which are used in connection with nouns).

lo (*l'*) = him *or* it (replacing a masculine noun in the singular).
la (*l'*) = her *or* it (replacing a feminine noun in the singular).
li = them (replacing masculine nouns in the plural).
le = them (replacing feminine nouns in the plural).

Lo, la, li, le always precede the verb. (But see p. 62.)

[1] *s* followed by a consonant.
[2] *Con* (with) lends itself less to this fusion, but *col, coi* are frequently used.

Quinta Lezione

suo padre sua madre suo padre sua madre

i suoi genitori i suoi genitori

mio cugino mia cugina

i loro figli

il bambino il ragazzo la ragazza

La Famiglia

A: *Un signore.* B: *Una signora.*

A (*mostrando*[1] *una fotografia dei suoi genitori**): Ecco mio padre* e mia madre.*

B (*guardando la fotografia*): Suo padre è alto,[2] non è vero?

A: Sì, è abbastanza[3] alto.

B: Sua madre non è alta come suo padre?

A: Essa è molto più p*i*ccola[4] di mio padre.

B: Quanti[5] fratelli[6] e quante sorelle ha (lei)?

A: Cinque. Tre fratelli e due sorelle. Ecco una fotograf*i*a dei miei genitori con tutti i loro figli.*

B: Chi è quella signora?

A: È la mia sorella maggiore.[7]

B: È sposata?[8]

A: Sì, è sposata da[9] sei anni.[10] Ecco una fotograf*i*a di mia sorella e dei suoi figli.

B: Quanti anni ha suo nipote?[11]

A: Ha quattro anni.

B: Va[12] già[13] a scuola?[14]

A: No, è ancora[15] troppo[16] gi*o*vane.[17]

B: E quanti anni ha sua nipote?[18]

A: Ha *u*ndici mesi.[19]

B: Allora[20] lei è lo zio[21] di questi bei[22] bambini?

A: Sì, sono il loro zio.

[1] mostrando, *showing.*
[2] alto, *tall.*
[3] abbastanza, *fairly.*
[4] più p*i*ccola, *smaller* (f.).
[5] quanti, –e, *how many.*
[6] il fratello, *brother.*
[7] maggiore, *elder.*
[8] sposata, *married.*
[9] da, *since.*
[10] sei anni, *six years.*
[11] il nipote, *nephew.*
[12] va, *he goes, he is going.*
[13] già, *already.*
[14] la scuola, *school.*
[15] ancora, *still.*
[16] troppo, *too.*
[17] gi*o*vane, *young.*
[18] la nipote, *niece.*
[19] il mese, *month.*
[20] allora, *so, therefore.*
[21] lo zio, *uncle.*
[22] bei (*from* bello), *beautiful.*

FLUENCY PRACTICE—see pp. 34–35

EXPLANATIONS

1. Both the familiar form of address (used when talking to children, relatives and close friends) and the polite form (used when talking to strangers, superiors or casual acquaintances) are different in the singular and in the plural.

Familiar Form:	SINGULAR	PLURAL
you have	(tu) hai	(voi) avete
you are	(tu) sei	(voi) siete
Polite Form:	SINGULAR	PLURAL
	(lei) ha	(loro) hanno
	(lei) è	(loro) sono

Note that the verb used in connection with the polite form of the pronoun is identical with the third person in both the singular and the plural.

2. *Possessive Adjectives*

	SINGULAR		PLURAL	
	masc.	*fem.*	*masc.*	*fem.*
My	il mio	la mia	i miei	le mie
Your (*fam. sing.*)	il tuo	la tua	i tuoi	le tue
Your (*pol. sing.*) / *His, her*	il suo	la sua	i suoi	le sue
Our	il nostro	la nostra	i nostri	le nostre
Your (*fam. pl.*)	il vostro	la vostra	i vostri	le vostre
Your (*pol. pl.*) / *Their*	il loro	la loro	i loro	le loro

The possessive adjectives are preceded by the article, except in front of singular nouns indicating relations (e.g. *mio fratello, mia sorella,* BUT *i miei fratelli, le mie sorelle*). When the singular noun is qualified by an adjective the article is inserted (*la mia sorella piccola,* my little sister). The words *babbo* (daddy) and *mamma* (mummy) also need the article.

Possessive adjectives in Italian agree with the noun expressing what is possessed and not (as in English) with the possessor, e.g. *il suo cappello* is the Italian for both 'his hat' and 'her hat', because *cappello* is masculine.

3. *Ecco* by itself can mean 'here is, here are, there is, there are'. To emphasise the difference between 'here' and 'there', *ecco* may be followed by *qui* for 'here is' and 'here are', and by *là* for 'there is' and 'there are'.

Note also: eccolo (qui), *here it is* (m.)
eccolo (là), *there it is* (m.)
eccoli (qui), *here they are* (m.)
eccoli (là), *there they are* (m.)
eccola (qui), *here it is* (f.)
eccola (là), *there it is* (f.)
eccole (qui), *here they are* (f.)
eccole (là), *there they are* (f.)

Fluency Practice

1.

Ecco		mio padre.	*Here (there) is*	*my father.*
		mia madre.		*my mother.*
Egli	è	mio fratello.	*He* | *is*	*my brother.*
Essa	non è	mia sorella.	*She* | *is not*	*my sister.*
		mio nipote.		*my nephew.*
		mia nipote.		*my niece.*

2.

Ecco		i miei genitori.	*Here* (*there*) *are*	*my parents.*
Essi	sono	i miei nonni.	*They* | *are*	*my grandparents.*
	non sono	i miei figli.	| *are not*	*my children.*
		i miei nipoti.		*my nephews.*

3.

Il mio	fazzoletto	è	rosso.	*My*	*handkerchief*	*is*	*red.*
Il tuo	colletto		grigio.	*Your* (fam.)[1]	*collar*		*grey.*
Il suo	cappello		bianco.	*His (or her)*	*hat*		*white.*
Il suo	ombrello		nero.	*Your* (polite)[1]	*umbrella*		*black.*
Il nostro	telefono		verde.	*Our*	*telephone*		*green.*
Il loro	pianoforte		marrone.	*Their*	*piano*		*brown.*
			giallo.				*yellow.*
			azzurro.				*blue.*

4.

La mia	cravatta	è	rossa.	*My*	*tie*	*is*	*red.*
La tua	cam*i*cia		gr*i*gia.	*Your* (fam.)	*shirt*		*grey.*
La sua	camicetta		bianca.	*His* (or *her*)	*blouse*		*white.*
La sua	borsetta		nera.	*Your* (pol.)	*handbag*		*black.*

[1] See Explanations 1 and 2.

5.

I miei	guanti	sono	nell'arm*a*dio.	*My*	*gloves*	*are*	*in the cupboard.*
I tuoi	occhiali	non sono	nel cassetto.	*Your* (fam. sing.)	*spectacles*	*are not*	*in the drawer.*
I suoi	pantaloni		nel cassettone.	*Your* (pol. sing.)	*trousers*		*in the chest-of-drawers.*
I suoi	cappelli		sotto la poltrona.	*His* (or *her*)	*hats*		*under the armchair.*
I nostri	fazzoletti		sul sofà.	*Our*	*handkerchiefs*		*on the sofa.*
I vostri			nell'antic*a*mera.	*Your* (fam. pl.)			*in the entrance-hall.*
I loro			nel ripost*i*glio.	*Your* (pol. pl.)			*in the box-room.*
I loro			nel salotto.	*Their*			*in the drawing-room.*

Le mie	scarpe	sono	nell'arm*a*dio.	*My*	*shoes*	*are*	*in the cupboard.*
Le tue	calze	non sono	nel cassetto.	*Your* (fam.)	*socks*	*are not*	*in the drawer.*
Le sue	cravatte		sul comodino.	*Your* (pol.)	*neckties*		*on the night-table.*
Le sue	cam*i*cie		sotto la poltrona.	*His* (or *her*)	*shirts*		*under the armchair.*
Le nostre	spazzole		sul sofà.	*Our*	*brushes*		*on the sofa.*
Le vostre			nell'antic*a*mera.	*Your* (fam.)			*in the entrance-hall.*
Le loro			nel ripost*i*glio.	*Your* (pol.)			*in the box-room.*
Le loro			nel salotto.	*Their*			*in the drawing-room.*

6.

Dov'è il mio ombrello?	*Where is my umbrella?*
È questo il suo ombrello?	*Is this your umbrella?*
*E*ccolo (qui).	*Here it* (m.) *is.*
*E*ccolo (là).	*There it* (m.) *is.*
Dov'è la mia val*i*gia?	*Where is my suitcase?*
Questa è la sua val*i*gia, non è vero?	*This is your suitcase, isn't it?*
*E*ccola (qui).	*Here it* (f.) *is.*
*E*ccola (là).	*There it* (f.) *is.*
Dove sono i miei guanti?	*Where are my gloves?*
Non sono qui.	*They are not here.*
Non sono nella tasca del suo sopr*a*bito?	*Aren't they in your overcoat pocket?*
Ah, *e*ccoli.	*Here they are.*
Com'è il suo sopr*a*bito?	*What is your overcoat like?*
È nero.	*It is black.*
Come sono le sue scarpe?	*What are your shoes like?*
Sono bianche.	*They are white.*
Dove sono le sue cravatte?	*Where are his neckties?*
*E*ccole qui.	*Here they are.*

Sesta Lezione

COLAZIONE

A: *Un signore.* B: *Il cameriere.*

(*Il cameriere bussa*[1] *alla porta della camera del signore.*)

A: Chi è?[2]

B: Sono io, il cameriere. Le porto la colazione.[3]

A: Entri!

B: Buongiorno, signore.

A: Buongiorno. Che cosa c'è per colazione?

B: Del caffè,* del latte,* dei panini* e del burro.*

A: Ma dov'è lo zucchero?* L'ha dimenticato?[4]

B: Oh, scusi, signore: l'ho dimenticato. Vado[5] a prenderlo[6] subito.[7]

(*Il cameriere esce,*[8] *e ritorna*[9] *poco dopo*[10] *con la zuccheriera.*[11])

[1] bussare, *to knock.*
[2] chi è, *who is there?*
[3] la colazione, *breakfast.*
[4] dimenticato, *forgotten.*
[5] vado, *I go.*
[6] prenderlo, *to bring it.*
[7] subito, *at once.*
[8] esce, *goes out.*
[9] ritorna, *comes back.*
[10] poco dopo, *soon afterwards.*
[11] la zuccheriera, *sugar-bowl.*

B: Ecco lo z*u*cchero. Quante[12] zolle[13] des*i*dera?

A: Due, per favore. Gr*a*zie. Che ore sono?[14]

B: Sono le otto e mezzo.[15]

A: A che ora arriva la posta?[16]

B: Verso[17] le otto. Vado a vedere[18] se c'è qualche cosa[19] per lei.

[12] quante, *how many.*
[13] la zolla, *lump.*
[14] Che ore sono? *What time is it?*
[15] otto e mezzo, *half-past eight.*
[16] la posta, *mail.*
[17] verso, *towards.*
[18] vedere, *to see.*
[19] qualche cosa, *something.*

Fluency Practice

1.

(Io)	mangio	del pane.	*I*	*eat*	*bread.*
(Lei)[1]	m*a*ngia	del burro.	*You*[1]		*butter.*
(Egli)		del form*a*ggio.	*He*	*eats*	*cheese.*
(Essa)		del dolce.	*She*		*dessert.*
Si[2]		della torta.	*One*[2]		*pie (tart, cake).*
(Noi)	mangiamo	della carne.	*We*	*eat*	*meat.*
(Loro)[1]	m*a*ngiano	della minestra.	*You*[1]		*soup.*
(Essi)		della verdura.	*They*		*vegetables.*
(Esse)		della frutta.			*fruit.*
		dell'insalata.			*salad.*
		dei biscotti.			*biscuits.*
		dei panini.			*rolls.*
		delle sardine.			*sardines.*

2.

(Io)	non m*a*ngio	pane.	*I*	*don't eat*	*bread.*
(Lei)	non m*a*ngia	burro.	*You*		*butter.*
(Egli)		form*a*ggio.	*He*	*doesn't eat*	*cheese.*
(Essa)		dolce.	*She*		*dessert.*
Non si m*a*ngia		carne.	*One*		*meat.*
(Noi)	non mangiamo	minestra.	*We*	*don't eat*	*soup.*
(Loro)	non m*a*ngiano	verdura.	*You*		*vegetables.*
(Essi)		frutta.	*They*		*fruit.*
(Esse)		insalata.			*salad.*
		biscotti.			*biscuits.*
		panini.			*rolls.*
		sardine.			*sardines.*

[1] The familiar forms are *tu mangi* and *voi mangiate.*
[2] also used in the sense of 'they (i.e. people) eat'.

3.	Non ho (io)	dello *zucchero*?	*Have I*	*no*	*sugar?*
	Non hai (tu)	del caffè?	*Have you*		*coffee?*
	Non ha (lei)	del latte?			*milk?*
	Non ha (egli)	della crema?	*Has he*		*custard?*
	Non ha (essa)	del vino?	*Has she*		*wine?*
	Non abbiamo (noi)	della birra?	*Have we*		*beer?*
	Non avete (voi)	delle arance?	*Have you*		*oranges?*
	Non hanno (loro)	delle pere?			*pears?*
	Non hanno (essi)	dei biscotti?	*Have they*		*biscuits?*
	Non hanno (esse)	della limonata?			*lemonade?*

4.	(Io)	ce l'ho.	*I*	*have it.*
		li ho.		*have them* (m.).
		le ho.		*have them* (f.).
		ne ho.		*have some.*
	(Io)	non ce l'ho.	*I*	*haven't got it.*
		non li ho.		*haven't got them* (m.).
		non le ho.		*haven't got them* (f.).
		non ne ho.		*haven't any.*

5.	(Lei)	ce l'ha.	*You*	*have it.*
		li ha.		*have them* (m.).
		le ha.		*have them* (f.).
		ne ha.		*have some.*
	Non	ce l'ha (lei)?		*Haven't you got it?*
		li ha (lei)?		*Haven't you got them* (m.)*?*
		le ha (lei)?		*Haven't you got them* (f.)*?*
		ne ha (lei)?		*Haven't you any?*

6.	(Noi)	ce l'abbiamo.	*We*	*have it.*
		li abbiamo.		*have them* (m.).
		le abbiamo.		*have them* (f.).
		ne abbiamo.		*have some.*
	(Noi)	non ce l'abbiamo.	*We*	*haven't got it.*
		non li abbiamo.		*haven't got them* (m.).
		non le abbiamo.		*haven't got them* (f.).
		non ne abbiamo.		*haven't any.*

7.	(Egli)	ce l'ha.	*He*	*has it.*
		li ha.		*has them* (m.).
		le ha.		*has them* (f.).
		ne ha.		*has some.*
	(Egli)	non ce l'ha.	*He*	*hasn't got it.*
		non li ha.		*hasn't got them* (m.).
		non le ha.		*hasn't got them* (f.).
		non ne ha.		*hasn't any.*
	(Essa)	ce l'ha.	*She*	*has it.*
		li ha.		*has them* (m.).
		le ha.		*has them* (f.).
		ne ha.		*has some.*

(Essa)	non ce l'ha. non li ha. non le ha. non ne ha.	*She*	*hasn't got it.* *hasn't got them* (m.). *hasn't got them* (f.). *hasn't any.*

8\.

(Essi) (Esse)	ce l'hanno. li hanno. le hanno. ne hanno.	*They* (m.) *They* (f.)	*have it.* *have them* (m.). *have them* (f.). *have some.*

Ce l'hanno (loro)?	*Have you got it?*
Li hanno (loro)?	*Have you got them* (m.)*?*
Le hanno (loro)?	*Have you got them* (f.)*?*
Ne hanno (loro)?	*Have you got some?*

9\. CHE ORA È? (CHE ORE SONO?) WHAT TIME IS IT?

È mezzogiorno.	*It is midday.*
È mezzanotte.	*It is midnight.*
È l'una.	*It is one o'clock.*
Sono le due.	*It is two o'clock.*
Sono le tre e cinque.	*It is five past three.*
Sono le quattro e dieci.	*It is ten past four.*
Sono le cinque e un quarto.	*It is a quarter past five.*
Sono le sei e venti.	*It is twenty past six.*
Sono le sette e mezzo.	*It is half past seven.*
Sono le otto meno venti.	*It is twenty to eight.*
Sono le nove meno un quarto.	*It is a quarter to nine.*
Sono le dieci meno cinque.	*It is five to ten.*
Sono le *u*ndici precise.	*It is exactly eleven o'clock.*

10\.

A che ora è la colazione?	*What time is breakfast?*
A che ora è il pranzo?	*What time is lunch?*
A che ora è la cena?	*What time is supper?*
A che ora parte il treno?	*At what time does the train leave?*
A che ora arriva la posta?	*At what time does the post arrive?*
C'è qualche cosa per me?	*Is there anything for me?*

EXPLANATIONS

1. *del* (a contraction of *di* + *il*) = some (*or* any), in front of a masculine noun in the singular.

   della = some (*or* any), in front of a feminine noun in the singular.

   dello = some (*or* any), in front of a masculine noun in the singular commencing with *s* impure or *z*.

   dell' = some (*or* any), in front of a noun in the singular commencing with a vowel.

dei = some (*or* any), in front of a masculine noun in the plural.

degli = some (*or* any), in front of a masculine noun in the plural commencing with a vowel, *s* impure or *z*.

delle = some (*or* any), in front of a feminine noun in the plural.

2. Distinguish between the following:
The definite article: *il, lo, la, i, gli, le.*
The indefinite article: *un, uno, una.*
The partitive article: *del, dello, della, dei, degli, delle.*

Nouns are generally preceded by one of these articles.

Where in English no article at all is used, as in 'We have meat for dinner', Italian uses the partitive articles, e.g. (*Noi*) *abbiamo della carne per il pranzo.* In negative sentences, however, or when the nouns are used in an indefinite or general sense the partitive is omitted, e.g.

Non m*a*ngio carne.	*I do not eat meat.*
Io vedo le *a*nitre.	*I see the ducks.*
Io vedo delle *a*nitre.	*I see some* (*a few*) *ducks.*
Io vedo *a*nitre.	*I see ducks* (*but no geese*).
Egli vende del tabacco.	*He sells tobacco* (*and other things*).
Egli vende tabacco.	*He sells tobacco* (*he is a tobacconist*).

3. *Ne* (some, any, of it, of them) replaces any noun used with the partitive article, e.g.

Ha delle sigarette?	*Have you got some cigarettes?*
Non ne ho.	*I haven't any.*

4. When the complement is *lo* or *la* (it), *ce* is sometimes used to strengthen the verb 'to have', in a manner similar to the use of *got* in 'I have got it': *io ce l'ho.*

5. *Lo ho* and *la ho,* 'I have it', are both contracted to *l'ho:* Io ce l'ho. *I have got it* (m. *or* f.).

Settima Lezione

della birra

un bicchiere di birra

una bott*i*glia di vino

del vino

una caraffa d'acqua

dell'acqua

AL CAFFÈ

A: *Un signore.* B: *Un signore.* C: *Il cameriere.*

A: Buongiorno, signor Bellini, come sta?[1]
B: Molto bene, gr*a*zie, e lei?
A: Non troppo[2] bene.
B: Che cos'ha?[3]
A: Un po' d'influenza. Come sta la sua signora?

[1] Come sta? *How are you?*
[2] troppo, *too.*
[3] che cosa, *what* (*the* a *may be omitted in front of* h *or a vowel*).

B: Mia moglie sta molto bene, la ringr*a*zio.[4]

A: E i suoi bambini, stanno bene?

B: Sono tutti[5] in buona salute,[6] gr*a*zie a Dio.

A: Vuol bere[7] qualche cosa con me?

B: Con piacere.

A: C'è un caffè di fronte.[8] Attraversiamo[9] la strada. (*Attraversano la via e si siedono*[10] *in un caffè.*)

C: Che cosa des*i*derano i signori?

A: Che cosa prende[11] lei?

B: Un bicchiere di birra.*

A: Io prendo una tazza di caffè.

C: Nero o con latte?

A: Con latte, per favore.

B: Come vanno gli affari?[12]

A: Vanno abbastanza[13] bene. E come vanno i suoi?

B: Non troppo bene.

A: Mi dispiace. Cameriere, il conto,[14] per favore.

C: Centocinquanta[15] lire la birra, e novanta[16] lire il caffè. Duecentoquaranta[17] lire, signore.

A: Non ho sp*i*ccioli.[18] Può[19] cambiarmi[20] un biglietto da mille lire?

C: Certamente, signore. Sessanta,[21] duecento,[22] e cinquecento,[23] che fanno mille.

A: (*dandogli*[24] *trenta lire*): Questo è per lei.

C: Gr*a*zie, signore. Arrivederci, signori.

[4] ringraziare, *to thank.*
[5] tutti, *all, everybody.*
[6] la salute, *health.*
[7] bere, *to drink.*
[8] di fronte, *opposite.*
[9] attraversiamo, *let us cross.*
[10] sedersi, *to sit down.*
[11] prendere, *to take.*
[12] gli affari, *business.*
[13] abbastanza, *fairly.*
[14] il conto, *bill.*
[15] centocinquanta, *one hundred and fifty.*
[16] novanta, *ninety.*
[17] duecentoquaranta, *two hundred and forty.*
[18] gli sp*i*ccioli, *small change.*
[19] può, *can you.*
[20] cambiarmi, *change me.*
[21] sessanta, *sixty.*
[22] duecento, *two hundred.*
[23] cinquecento, *five hundred.*
[24] d*a*ndogli, *giving him.*

Fluency Practice

1.

I signori	*e*ntrano.	*The gentlemen*	*are*	*coming in.*[1]
Le signore	s*a*lgono.	*The ladies*		*coming up.*
I ragazzi	rit*o*rnano.	*The boys*		*coming back.*
Le ragazze	lav*o*rano.	*The girls*		*working.*
Gli insegnanti	gi*o*cano.	*The teachers*		*playing.*
Gli allievi	*e*scono.	*The pupils*		*going out.*

2.

Sono (essi)	i ministri	*Are they*	*the ministers*
Non sono (essi)	gli attori	*Aren't they*	*the actors*
Sì, (essi) sono	i portal*e*ttere	*Yes, they are*	*the postmen*
No, (essi) non sono	i pompieri	*No, they aren't*	*the firemen*

3.

*E*ntrano	i ragazzi?	*Are the boys*	*coming*[1] *in?*
Rit*o*rnano	i pompieri?	*Are the firemen*	*coming back?*

Sì, (essi)	*e*ntrano.	*Yes, they are*	*coming*[1] *in.*
No, (essi) non	rit*o*rnano.	*No, they are not*	*coming back.*

4.

(Io) sto	bene.	*I am*	*well.*
(Tu) stai	ben*i*ssimo.	*You*[3] *are*	*very well.*
(Egli) sta	male.	*He is*	*ill.*
(Noi) stiamo	abbastanza bene.	*We are*	*fairly well.*
(Voi) state	sempre bene.	*You*[5] *are*	*always well.*
(Essi) stanno	mal*i*ssimo.	*They*[6] *are*	*very ill.*

5.

(Io) vengo		dal teatro.	*I*	*come*[2]	*from the theatre.*
(Tu) vieni		dal c*i*nema.	*You*[3]		*from the cinema.*
(Lei)	viene	dal caffè.	*You*[4]		*from the café.*
(Egli)		dalla stazione.	*He*	*comes*	*from the station.*
(Essa)		dalla posta.	*She*		*from the post.*
(Noi) veniamo		dalla biblioteca.	*We*	*come*	*from the library.*
(Voi) venite		dalla scuola.	*You*[5]		*from the school.*
(Loro)	vengono		*You*[6]		
(Essi)			*They*[7]		
(Esse)			*They*[8]		

[1] or *going in.*
[2] or *am coming,* etc.
[3] familiar form, singular.
[4] polite form, singular.
[5] familiar form, plural.
[6] polite form, plural.
[7] masculine.
[8] feminine.

6. È	il cappello	di Giovanni.	*It is*	*John's*	*hat.*
	l'ombrello	di Maria.		*Mary's*	*umbrella.*
	la val*i*gia	dell'insegnante.		*the teacher's*	*suitcase.*
	l'orol*o*gio	del prete.		*the priest's*	*watch.*
	il portaf*o*glio	del banchiere.		*the banker's*	*wallet.*
	il passaporto	dell'allievo.		*the pupil's*	*passport.*
	la casa	dello studente.		*the student's*	*house.*

Sono	i guanti	degli insegnanti.	*They are*	*the teachers'*	*gloves.*
	i libri	dei banchieri.		*the bankers'*	*books.*
	le foto-graf*i*e	di Giovanni e di Maria.		*John's and Mary's*	*photographs.*

7.	(Io) vado	a scuola.	*I am*	*going*	*to school.*
	(Tu) vai	a teatro.	*You*[1] *are*		*to the theatre.*
	(Lei) va	al c*i*nema.	*You*[2] *are*		*to the cinema.*
	(Egli)	al caffè.	*He is*		*to the café.*
	(Essa)	alla stazione.	*She is*		*to the station.*
	(Noi) andiamo	alla posta.	*We are*		*to the post-office.*
	(Voi) andate	alla farmacia.	*You*[3] *are*		*to the chemist.*
	(Loro) vanno	in chiesa.	*You*[4] *are*		*to church.*
	(Essi)	in campagna	*They*[5] *are*		*to the country.*
	(Esse)	al mare.	*They*[6] *are*		*to the seaside.*

(Io) prendo	del tè.
(Tu) prendi	della birra.
(Lei) prende	un succo di frutta.
(Egli)	un bicchiere grande di vino rosso.
(Essa)	una bott*i*glia grande di birra chiara.
(Noi) prendiamo	una bott*i*glia p*i*ccola di birra scura.
(Voi) prendete	una tazza di caffelatte.
(Loro) pr*e*ndono	un 'cappuccino'.
(Essi)	un'aranciata.
(Esse)	un gelato.

I am taking	(*some*) *tea.*
You[1] *are taking*	(*some*) *beer.*
You[2] *are taking*	*a fruit juice.*
He is taking	*a large glass of red wine.*
She is taking	*a large bottle of light beer.*
We are taking	*a small bottle of dark beer.*
You[3] *are taking*	*a cup of white coffee.*
You[4] *are taking*	*coffee with a drop of milk.*
They[5] *are taking*	*an orange squash.*
They[6] *are taking*	*an ice-cream.*

[1] familiar form, singular.
[2] polite form, singular.
[3] familiar form, plural.
[4] polite form, plural.
[5] masculine.
[6] feminine.

1. A verb consists of two elements: the stem and the ending. The stem is invariable in regular verbs, while the ending undergoes certain variations by which persons, tenses and moods are distinguished.

Italian verbs are divided into three conjugations according to whether the infinitive ends in *–are, –ere* or *–ire*, e.g.

mangi*are* (to eat), vend*ere* (to sell), part*ire* (to leave).

Each conjugation has a pattern of its own. The verbs which follow a pattern are regular and those which do not are irregular. For instance, *venire* (to come) is an irregular verb (see Fluency Practice).

The regular patterns for the Present Tense of the three conjugations are:

In connection with		*Verbs ending in –are*	*Verbs ending in –ere*	*Verbs ending in –ire*
io*	*they end in*	–o (m*a*ngio)	–o (vendo)	–o (parto)
tu*	,,	–i (mangi)	–i (vendi)	–i (parti)
lei,* egli,* esso,* essa*	,,	–a (m*a*ngia)	–e (vende)	–e (parte)
noi*	,,	–iamo (mangiamo)	–iamo (vendiamo)	–iamo (partiamo)
voi*	,,	–ate (mangiate)	–ete (vendete)	–ite (partite)
loro,* essi,* esse*	,,	–ano (m*a*ngiano)	–ono (vendono)	–ono (p*a*rtono)

In the 1st, 2nd and 3rd persons singular and in the 3rd person plural many verbs in *–ire* assume the endings *–isco, –isci, –isce, –iscono,* instead of *–o, –i, –e, –ono*, e.g.

FINIRE, to end

io fin*isco*	noi finiamo
tu fin*isci*	voi finite
lei, egli fin*isce*	loro, essi fin*iscono.*

2. There is no equivalent in Italian to the English possessive case ending in *'s*. 'The baker's wife' is 'the wife of the baker' (*la moglie del panettiere*). 'Anne's pretty frock' is 'the pretty frock of Anne' (*il bel vestito di Anna*).

* May be omitted.

Ottava Lezione

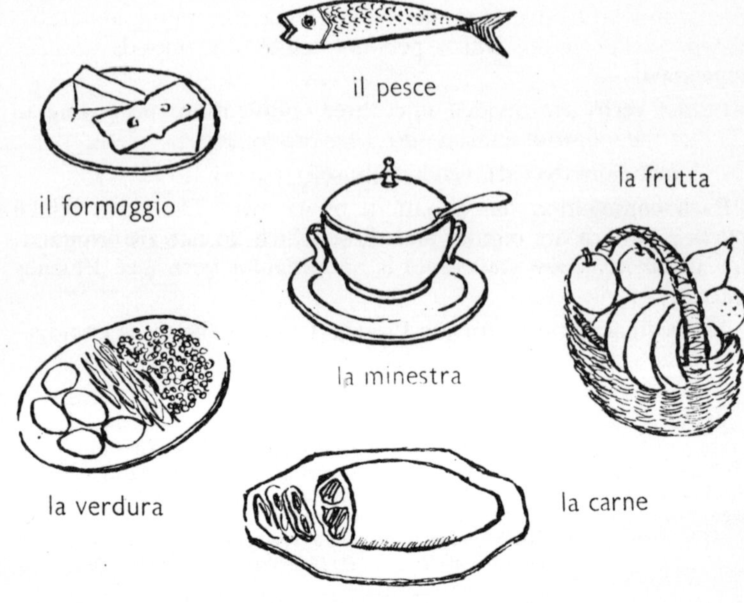

Al Ristorante

A: *Un signore.* B: *Una signorina.* C: *Il cameriere.*

C: Ecco il menù.

A: Prende la minestra?*

B: No, non m*a*ngio mai[1] la minestra a pranzo.[2]

A: Nemmeno io.[3] Che cosa c'è per antipasto?[4]

C: Delle sardine, dei filetti di aringa,[5] del salame, del prosciutto,[6] dei ravanelli,[7] delle olive e delle bi*e*tole.[8]

B: Io prendo del prosciutto.

A: Per me delle sardine e delle olive.

[1] non m*a*ngio mai, *I never eat.*
[2] il pranzo, *lunch.*
[3] nemmeno io, *neither do I.*
[4] un antipasto, *hors d'œuvre.*
[5] i filetti di aringa, *herring fillets.*
[6] il prosciutto, *ham.*
[7] i ravanelli, *radishes.*
[8] le bi*e*tole, *beetroots.*

C: E dopo,[9] che cosa des*i*derano? Del pesce,* della carne?*

A: Porti intanto[10] l'antipasto. Ci lasci[11] il menù.

C: Va bene, signore.

A: M*a*ngia del pesce, lei? Ci sono delle trote[12] e delle s*o*gliole[13] al burro.[14]

B: No, non prendo pesce; prenderò della carne. Che carne c'è?

A: Del vitello,[15] dell'arrosto,[16] delle cotolette[17] di maiale.[18]. C'è anche del pollo[19] e della selvaggina.[20]

B: Lei che cosa prende?

A: Io prendo dell'arrosto. È una specialità di questo ristorante.

B: Allora lo prendo anch'io.[21]

A: E come verdura,[22] un'insalata di lattuga?[23]

B: D'accordo.[24]

[9] dopo, *then, afterwards.*
[10] intanto, *meanwhile.*
[11] ci lasci, *leave us.*
[12] trota, *trout.*
[13] la s*o*gliola, *sole.*
[14] il burro, *butter.*
[15] il vitello, *veal.*
[16] l'arrosto, *roast* (*beef*).
[17] la cotoletta, *chop.*
[18] il maiale, *pork.*
[19] il pollo, *chicken.*
[20] la selvaggina, *game.*
[21] anch'io, *I too.*
[22] e come verdura, *and for vegetables.*
[23] la lattuga, *lettuce.*
[24] d'accordo (*short for* io sono d'accordo), *I agree.*

Explanations

1. Words denoting quantity (e.g. *molto*, much; *troppo*, too much; *poco*, little) can be used as adverbs (in connection with verbs) or adjectives (qualifying nouns). When adverbs they are invariable; but when used as adjectives, they have to agree with the gender and number of the noun they qualify. *Abbastanza*, 'enough', is invariable.

2. The future tense of verbs is formed by adding certain endings to the infinitive, which drops the final *–e*. These endings are the same for all verbs: *–ò*, *–ai*, *–à*, *–emo*, *–ete*, *–anno*. Verbs of the first conjugation change the *a* of the infinitive ending *–are* into *e*: *mangiare* (to eat); *mangerò*, I shall eat.

3. *Io ho fame*, I am hungry (lit. I have hunger).

'To be hungry, thirsty, sleepy, cold, afraid', are expressed by 'to have hunger, thirst', etc.

Fluency Practice

1.

(Io) m*a*ngio	molto	pane.	*I eat*	*much*	*bread.*
(Tu) mangi	troppo	form*a*ggio.	*You*[1] *eat*	*too much*	*cheese.*
(Lei) m*a*ngia	poco	pesce.	*You*[2] *eat*	*little*	*fish.*
(Egli) m*a*ngia	abbastanza	cioccolato.	*He eats*	*enough*	*chocolate.*
(Essa) m*a*ngia			*She eats*		
(Noi) mangiamo	molta	carne.	*We eat*		*meat.*
(Voi) mangiate	troppa	verdura.	*You*[3] *eat*		*vegetables.*
(Loro) m*a*ngiano	poca	frutta.	*You*[4] *eat*		*fruit.*
(Essi) m*a*ngiano	abbastanza	panna montata.	*They*[5] *eat*		*whipped cream.*
(Esse) m*a*ngiano			*They*[6] *eat*		

2.

(Io) bevo	del tè.	*I drink*	*tea.*
(Tu) bevi	del caffè.	*You*[1] *drink*	*coffee.*
(Lei) beve	del cacao.	*You*[2] *drink*	*cocoa.*
(Egli) beve	della birra.	*He drinks*	*beer.*
(Essa) beve	della limonata.	*She drinks*	*lemonade.*
(Noi) beviamo	dell'aranciata.	*We drink*	*orangeade.*
(Voi) bevete	del succo di frutta.	*You*[3] *drink*	*fruit juice.*
(Loro) b*e*vono	del succo d'ar*a*ncia	*You*[4] *drink*	*orange juice.*
(Essi) b*e*vono	del succo di pomodoro.	*They*[5] *drink*	*tomato juice.*
(Esse) b*e*vono	del vino.	*They*[6] *drink*	*wine.*

3.

A colazione	(io) prendo	un uovo sodo.	*For breakfast*	*I take*	*a hard boiled egg.*
A pranzo	(tu) prendi	delle uova strapazzate.	*For dinner*	*you*[1] *take*	*scrambled eggs.*
A cena	(lei) prende	delle uova al burro.	*For supper*	*you*[2] *take*	*fried eggs.*
Per antipasto	(egli) prende	una frittata di funghi.	*As hors d'œuvre*	*he takes*	*a mushroom omelette.*
Per dolce	(essa) prende	della minestra in brodo.	*As a sweet*	*she takes*	*clear soup.*
Per cominciare	(noi) prendiamo	un'insalata di cetrioli.	*To begin*	*we take*	*a cucumber salad.*
Poi	(voi) prendete	del gelato alla fr*a*gola.	*Then*	*you*[3] *take*	*a strawberry ice.*
Per finire	(loro) pr*e*ndono	dell'antipasto.	*To finish*	*you*[4] *take*	*hors d'œuvre.*
	(essi) pr*e*ndono	della crostata di mele.		*they*[5] *take*	*some apple pie.*
	(esse) pr*e*ndono	delle banane.		*they*[6] *take*	*some bananas.*

[1] familiar singular. [2] polite singular. [3] familiar plural. [4] polite plural. [5] masculine. [6] feminine.

4.

Subject	Verb	Object				
(Io)	mangerò prenderò	del pesce	*I shall*		*eat* *take*	*fish.*
		dell'arrosto.				*roast.*
		della minestra.				*soup.*
(Tu)	mangerai prenderai	della carne.	*You*[1]	*will*		*meat.*
		dell'insalata.				*salad.*
		della verdura.				*vegetables.*
		della frutta.				*fruit.*
(Lei) (Egli) (Essa)	mangerà prenderà	dei piselli.	*You*[2] *He* *She*			*peas.*
		dei fagiolini.				*French beans.*
		degli spinaci.				*spinach.*
		delle patate.				*potatoes.*
(Noi)	mangeremo prenderemo	delle carote.	*We shall*			*carrots.*
		degli zucchini.				*baby marrows.*
		delle cipolle.				*onions.*
(Voi)	mangerete prenderete	dei peperoni.	*You*[3]	*will*		*peppers.*
		dei cavolfiori.				*cauliflowers.*
		dei cavoli.				*cabbage.*
(Loro) (Essi) (Esse)	mangeranno prenderanno		*You*[4] *They*[5] *They*[6]			

5.

Subject	Verb	Object			
(Io)	ho	fame.	*I*	*am*	*hungry.*
(Tu)	hai	sete.	*You*[1]	*are*	*thirsty.*
(Lei) (Egli) (Essa)	ha	caldo.	*You*[2]	*are*	*warm.*
		freddo.	*He* *She*	*is*	*cold.*
		ragione.			*right.*
		torto.			*wrong.*
(Noi)	abbiamo	sonno.	*We*	*are*	*sleepy.*
(Voi)	avete		*You*[3]		
(Loro) (Essi) (Esse)	hanno		*You*[4] *They*[5] *They*[6]		

[1] familiar singular. [2] polite singular. [3] familiar plural. [4] polite plural. [5] masculine. [6] feminine.

6.

Subject	Verb	Place	Time
(Io)	sarò / andrò	a Roma	questa sera.
(Tu)	sarai / andrai	in Italia	domani.
(Egli) (Essa)	sarà / andrà	in Inghilterra	dopo domani.
(Noi)	saremo / andremo	in Scozia	lunedì prossimo.
(Voi)	sarete / andrete	in Germania	la settimana prossima.
(Essi) (Esse)	saranno / andranno	in Svizzera	fra una settimana.
		in Danimarca	fra quindici giorni.
		in Russia	il mese prossimo.
		negli Stati Uniti	fra un mese.

I shall be in	*Rome*	*this evening.*
I shall go to	*Italy*	*tomorrow.*
You[1] will be in	*England*	*the day after tomorrow.*
You[1] will go to	*Scotland*	*next Monday.*
He will be in	*Germany*	*next week.*
She will go to	*Switzerland*	*in a week.*
We shall be in	*Denmark*	*in a fortnight.*
We shall go to	*Russia*	*next month.*
You[3] will be in	*the United States*	*in a month's time.*
You[3] will go to		
They[5] will be in		
They[6] will go to		

7.

Questo / Il mio / Il suo	orologio / ombrello / cappello	è	d'oro.
Questa / La mia / La sua	chiave / penna / matita	è	d'argento.
Questi / I miei / I suoi / I vostri / I loro	guanti / colletti / cucchiai / anelli / orecchini	sono	di ferro.
Queste / Le mie / Le sue / Le vostre / Le loro	scarpe / calze / forchette / posate / bottiglie	sono	d'acciaio.
			di vetro.
			di nichel.
			di seta.
			di lana.
			di cotone.
			di tela.
			di pelle.
			di nailon.
			di carta.
			di plastica.
			di feltro.
			di paglia.
			di legno.
			di madreperla.

This / My / His/her/your[2]	*watch / umbrella / hat*	*is*	*(made) of gold.*
This / My / His/her/your[2]	*key / pen / pencil*	*is*	*silver.*
These / My / His/her/your[2] / Your[3] / Their/your[4]	*gloves / collars / spoons / rings / ear-rings*	*are*	*iron.*
These / My / His/her/your[2] / Your[3] / Their/your[4]	*shoes / socks / forks / cutlery / bottles*	*are*	*steel.*
			glass.
			nickel.
			silk.
			wool.
			cotton.
			linen.
			leather.
			nylon.
			paper.
			plastic.
			felt.
			straw.
			wood.
			mother-of-pearl.

[1] familiar singular. [2] polite singular. [3] familiar plural. [4] polite plural. [5] masculine. [6] feminine.

Nona Lezione

una bicicletta

uno scooter
(una motoretta)

una motocicletta

un autocarro

un'autom*o*bile

un *a*utobus

ALLA FERMATA DELL'*A*UTOBUS

A: *Primo signore.* B: *Secondo signore.* C: *Terzo signore.*
D: *Il bigliettario* (conductor) *del primo autobus.*
E: *Il bigliettario del secondo autobus.*

A: È lontano[1] da qui corso Garibaldi?

B: Circa[2] un quarto d'ora a piedi.[3] Può pr*e*ndere o[4] l'*a*utobus o[4] il tram.

A: Preferisco l'*a*utobus.

B: C'è una fermata[5] qui vicino. Volti[6] a sinistra e percorra[7] la via fino al[8] sem*a*foro.[9] Attraversi la piazza e continui fino alla

[1] lontano, *far*
[2] circa, *about*.
[3] a piedi, *on foot*.
[4] o...o, *either...or*.
[5] la fermata, *stop*.
[6] voltare, *to turn*.
[7] percorrere, *to go along*.
[8] fino al, *as far as, until*.
[9] il sem*a*foro, *traffic lights*.

seconda via a destra. Prenda quella via e troverà[10] la fermata dell'*a*utobus alla sua sinistra.

A: Che *a*utobus devo[11] pr*e*ndere?

B: Il n*u*mero sette; lo porterà direttamente in corso Garibaldi.

A: Molte gr*a*zie. Buongiorno.

. . . . . .

A: È questa la fermata per andare in corso Garibaldi?

C: Sì, è questa. Prenda il n*u*mero 7. Ecco l'*a*utobus che arriva.

. . . . . .

D: Avanti,[12] signori. Ora è completo;[13] non c'è più[14] posto.[15]

C: Ecco un altro *a*utobus. Ci sono molti posti qui.[16] Salga,[17] prego. (*Salgono sull'autobus.*)

E: Avanti, signori; in fondo[18] c'è posto.

[10] trovare, *to find.*
[11] devo, *I must.*
[12] avanti, *right inside.*
[13] completo, *full up.*
[14] non...più, *no more.*
[15] il posto, *room, place.*
[16] qui, *here.*
[17] salga, *get in.*
[18] in fondo, *at the end.*

Fluency Practice

1.

È	un bel parco.	*It is*	*a beautiful park.*
	un bell'uccello.		*a beautiful bird.*
	un bello scherzo.		*a good joke.*
	un bella borsetta.		*a beautiful handbag.*
	una buona idea.		*a good idea.*
	un buon albergo.		*a good hotel.*
	un v*e*cchio castello.		*an old castle.*
	una grande casa.		*a big house.*
	un gi*o*vane studente.		*a young student.*
	un nuovo insegnante.		*a new teacher.*
	una donna intelligente.		*an intelligent woman.*
	una matita rossa.		*a red pencil.*
	un dizion*a*rio italiano.		*an Italian dictionary.*

2.

Sono	dei buoni amici.	*They are*	*good friends.*
	dei bei colori.		*beautiful colours.*
	dei begli occhi.		*beautiful eyes.*
	dei nuovi studenti.		*new students.*
	delle cattive abit*u*dini.		*bad habits.*
	dei libri divertenti.		*amusing books.*
	dei gatti bianchi.		*white cats.*
	degli studenti canadesi.		*Canadian students.*

3.

È	molto	f*a*cile.
	così	diff*i*cile.
	piuttosto	lungo(a).
	troppo	corto(a).
	abbastanza	grosso(a).
	un po'	sottile.
		spesso(a).
		largo(a).
		stretto(a).

It is	*very*	*easy.*
	so	*difficult.*
	rather	*long.*
	too	*short.*
	fairly	*big.*
	a little	*thin.*
		thick.
		broad.
		narrow.

4.

Sulla t*a*vola	c'è	del gesso.
Nel cassetto		della carta.

CE N'È.

There is	*chalk*	*on the table.*
	paper	*in the drawer.*

There is some.

Sulla t*a*vola	ci sono	dei libri.
Sotto il giornale		delle buste.

CE NE SONO.

There are	*books*	*on the table.*
	envelopes	*under the newspaper.*

There are some.

Nella mia tazza	non c'è	caffè.
Sulla t*a*vola		latte.
In casa		z*u*cchero.

NON CE N'È.

There is no	*coffee*	*in my cup.*
	milk	*on the table.*
	sugar	*at home.*

There isn't any.

Sulla t*a*vola	non ci sono	piatti.
Nella credenza		coltelli.
		forchette.

NON CE NE SONO.

There are no	*dishes*	*on the table.*
	knives	*in the cupboard.*
	forks	

There aren't any.

5.

(Io) ho già	del pane	ma non ho	biscotti.
	della carne		sale.
	delle sigarette		fiamm*i*feri.
	del burro		marmellata.
	della birra		bicchieri.
	del prosciutto		piatti.
(Io) ne ho già			

I already have some	*bread*	*but I haven't any*	*biscuits.*
	meat		*salt.*
	cigarettes		*matches.*
	butter		*jam* (or *marmalade*).
	beer		*glasses.*
	ham		*plates.*
I already have some			

6.

(Io)	posso *v*oglio devo (debbo)	salire. sc*e*ndere. continuare. pr*e*ndere l'*a*utobus. andarci. attraversare la strada. farlo. uscire. entrare. sentirlo. vederla. scrivergli. parlarle. saperlo. lasciarla. aspettarli. pagarle. domandare.
(Tu)	puoi vuoi devi	
(Lei) (Egli) (Essa)	può vuole deve	
(Noi)	possiamo vogliamo dobbiamo	
(Voi)	potete volete dovete	
(Loro) (Essi) (Esse)	p*o*ssono v*o*gliono d*e*vono (d*e*bbono)	

I *You* (fam. sing.)	*can* *wish to* *have to*	*get in* (or *up*). *get off* (or *down*). *go on.* *take the bus.* *go there.* *cross the road.* *do it.* *go out.* *come in.* *hear him.* *see her.* *write to him.* *speak to her.* *know* (*it*). *leave her.* *wait for them.* *pay them* (f. pl.) *ask.*
You (pol. sing.) *He* *She*	*can* *wishes to* *has to*	
We *You* (fam. pl.) *You* (pl.) *They* (m.) *They* (f.)	*can* *wish to* *have to*	

7.

È	vicino	alla fermata? al caffè? all'albergo? alla stazione?
	lontano	da qui? di là? dal caffè? dall'albergo? dalla stazione?

Is it	*near*	*the stop?* *the café?* *the hotel?* *the station?*
	far from	*here?* *there?* *the café?* *the hotel?* *the station?*

8.					
Quale *a*utobus	devo	prendere?	*Which bus*	*must I*	*take?*
Quale via	dobbiamo		*Which road*	*must we*	

Quali sigarette	preferisce?	*Which cigarettes*	*do you prefer?*
Quali s*i*gari	des*i*dera?	*Which cigars*	*would you like?*

9.					
Il primo	cappello	blu.	*The first*	*blue*	*hat.*
L'*u*ltimo	cappotto	marrone.	*The last*	*brown*	*overcoat.*
Il solo	vestito	nero.	*The only*	*black*	*dress.*
Lo stesso	*a*bito	bianco.	*The same*	*white*	*costume.*
L'altro	completo	rosso.	*The other*	*red*	*suit.*
Un buon	panciotto	gr*i*gio.	*A good*	*grey*	*waistcoat.*
Un altro	ombrello	p*i*ccolo.	*Another (different one)*	*small*	*umbrella.*
	lenzuolo	grande.		*big*	*sheet.*
Ancora un	asciuga-mano	nuovo.	*Another (an additional one)*	*new*	*hand-towel.*
Il miglior(e)			*The best*		

10.					
La prima	cravatta	blu.	*The first*	*blue*	*tie.*
L'*u*ltima	giacca	marrone.	*The last*	*brown*	*jacket.*
La sola	cam*i*cia	nera.	*The only*	*black*	*shirt.*
La stessa	camicetta	bianca.	*The same*	*white*	*blouse.*
L'altra	gonna	rossa.	*The other*	*red*	*skirt.*
Una buona	m*a*glia	gr*i*gia.	*A good*	*grey*	*pullover.*
Un'altra	coperta	p*i*ccola.	*Another (different one)*	*small*	*blanket.*
	val*i*gia	grande.		*big*	*suitcase.*
Ancora una		nuova.	*Another (an additional one)*	*new*	
La miglior(e)			*The best*		

EXPLANATIONS

1. We have already noticed that adjectives usually follow the noun, but that certain short common adjectives like *bello, buono, vecchio, giovane, grande* precede it.

On the other hand, adjectives denoting colour, shape, nationality and religion always follow the noun.

2. *Quale* = which, when followed by a singular noun.
Quali = which, when followed by a plural noun.

3. *Quanto* = how much (*m.*)
Quanta = how much (*f.*)
Quanti = how many (*m.*)
Quante = how many (*f.*)

4. The comparison of the adjective is formed with the word *più*, e.g.

più intelligente di, *more intelligent than*
più grosso di, *larger than*

'Than' after a comparison is *di*.

The superlative is formed with *più* preceded by the appropriate article, e.g.

il più bello
la più bella
i più belli
le più belle } *the most beautiful*

The comparison of inferiority is formed with *meno*, and *il* (*la, i, le*) *meno* is used for the superlative, e.g.

meno brutto, *less ugly*
il meno brutto, *the least ugly*

'Very' before an adjective is often expressed by dropping the final vowel of the adjective and adding –i*ssimo*, obtaining the form of the *superlativo assoluto*, e.g.

svelto, *quick*: svelt*i*ssimo, *very quick*

Irregular comparatives and superlatives are:

buono,	migliore,	il migliore,	ottimo,	*good,*	*better,*	*best,*	*excellent*
cattivo,	peggiore,	il peggiore,	pessimo,	*bad,*	*worse*	*worst,*	*very bad*
grande,	maggiore,	il maggiore,	massimo,	*great,*	*greater,*	*greatest,*	*very great*
piccolo,	minore,	il minore,	minimo,	*little,*	*less,*	*least,*	*the least*

5. Adverbs derived from adjectives are formed by adding *–mente* to the feminine form of the adjective, e.g.

generoso, generosamente, *generous, generously*

allegro, allegramente, *merry, merrily*

Exceptions:

buono, bene, *good, well*

cattivo, male, *bad, badly*

Adverbs form their comparison in the same way as adjectives, e.g.

facilmente, più facilmente, *easily, more easily*
il più facilmente, *most easily*

A few adverbs have an irregular comparison:

bene	meglio	il meglio	*well*	*better*	*the best*
male	peggio	il peggio	*badly*	*worse*	*the worst*
molto	più	il più	*much*	*more*	*the most*
poco	meno	il meno	*little*	*less*	*the least*

Il meglio, il peggio, il più, il meno are used only as nouns, e.g.

Il meglio che possa succedermi...*The best that can happen to me...*

Sometimes adjectives are used as adverbs, e.g.

parliamoci chiaro, *let us be frank*
parla forte, *speak loudly*
camminate piano, *walk slowly*

The adverb *oggi* (today) can be reinforced by combining it with *questo: quest'oggi.* Other combinations with *oggi* are: *oggigiorno* or *al giorno d'oggi* (nowadays). *Mattina* can be combined with *questa,* becoming *stamattina* or *stamani* (this morning). Similarly *questa sera* can be shortened into *stasera* (this evening).

Decima Lezione

(Egli) è in piedi.

(Egli) è seduto.

(Essa) è in piedi.

(Essa) è seduta.

NELL'AUTOBUS

A: *Un signore.* B: *Un altro signore.* C: *Il bigliettario.*

C: Biglietti, per favore.
A: Corso Garibaldi, per piacere.
C: Cinquanta lire.
A: Può cambiare[1] un biglietto da mille lire?
C: Ora guardo.[2] Lei è fortunato: ecco il resto[3] delle mille lire.

[1] cambiare, *to change.*
[2] ora guardo, *let me see* (*lit. now I look*).
[3] il resto, *change.*

A (*ad un signore*): Mi scusi, potrebbe[4] dirmi che cos'è quel bell'edi*fi*cio?[5]

B: È il palazzo delle Poste. A destra può vedere via Pen*i*sola, la più elegante della città. In fondo a via Pen*i*sola si vede[6] il monumento a Marconi.

A: L'ho visto[7] ieri;[8] è davvero imponente.[9] È ancora[10] lontano[11] corso Garibaldi?

B: Non molto. Ci saranno ancora due o tre fermate.

A: Devo sc*e*ndere[12] qui?

B: Sì. Corso Garibaldi incom*i*ncia[13] dalla parte opposta della piazza.[14]

A: Gr*a*zie mille.[15]

[4] potrebbe, *could you.*
[5] un edi*fi*cio, *building.*
[6] si vede, *one sees, one can see.*
[7] visto, *seen.*
[8] ieri, *yesterday.*
[9] imponente, *imposing.*
[10] ancora, *still.*
[11] lontano, *far.*
[12] sc*e*ndere, *to get off.*
[13] incominciare, *to start.*
[14] la piazza, *square.*
[15] gr*a*zie mille, *many thanks.*

Fluency Practice

1.

Parli	al direttore.	*Speak to*	*the manager.*
Risponda	all'incaricato.	*Reply to*	*the man in charge.*
Domandi	alle signore.	*Ask*	*the ladies.*
Dica	ai signori.	*Tell*	*the gentlemen.*
Scriva	loro.	*Write to*	*them.*

Mi	parli.	*Speak to*	*me.*
Gli	risponda.	*Reply to*	*him.*
Le	domandi.	*Ask*	*her.*
Ci	dica.	*Tell*	*us.*

2.

Non	mi	parli.	*Don't*	*speak*	*to me.*
	ci	risponda.		*reply*	*to us.*
	gli	domandi.		*ask*	*him.*
	le	dica nulla.		*tell*	*her anything.*

Non risponda loro. — *Don't answer them.*

3.

(Io)	gli	parlo.	*I*	*speak to*	*him.*
	le	domando.		*ask*	*her.*
	vi	dico.		*tell*	*you.*

(Io) rispondo loro. — *I answer them.*

4.

(Egli)	mi	parla.
(Essa)	gli	domanda.
	le	sorride.
	ci	scrive.
	vi	tel*e*fona.

He	*speaks to*	*me.*
She	*asks*	*him.*
	smiles at	*you* (sing.)/*her.*
	writes to	*us.*
	rings	*you* (pl.).

(Egli)	risponde loro.
(Essa)	non parla loro.

He	*answers them.*
She	*doesn't speak to them.*

5.

(Essi)	mi	p*a*rlano.
(Esse)	ci	dom*a*ndano.
	vi	sorr*i*dono.
	gli	scr*i*vono.
	le	tel*e*fonano.

They	*speak to*	*me.*
	ask	*us.*
	smile at	*you* (pl.).
	write to	*him.*
	ring	*you* (sing.)/*her.*

(Essi)	risp*o*ndono loro.
(Esse)	non p*a*rlano loro.

They	*answer them.*
	do not speak to them.

6.

Parliamo	al signore.
Rispondiamo	alla signora.
Scriviamo	al direttore.

Let us	*speak to*	*the gentleman.*
	reply to	*the lady.*
	write to	*the manager.*

Domandi*a*mogli.
Rispondi*a*mole.
Diciamo loro.

Let us	*ask him.*
	answer her.
	tell them.

Non	parliamo	a quest'uomo.
	scriviamo	a quella donna.

Don't let us	*speak*	*to this man.*
	write	*to that woman.*

Non	parli*a*mogli.
	scrivi*a*mole.
	rispondiamo loro.

Don't let us	*speak to him.*
	write to her.
	answer them.

7.

V*o*glio	farlo.
So	ascoltarlo.
Posso	vederlo.
Devo	cercarlo.
Des*i*dero	incominciarlo.
Sto per	finirlo.

I want to	*do it.*
I know how to	*listen to it.*
I can	*see it.*
I have to	*look for it.*
I wish to	*start it.*
I am about to	*finish it.*

Vuole	farlo?
Sa	incominciarlo?
Può	finirlo?

Do you want to	*do it?*
Do you know how to	*start it?*
Can you	*finish it?*

8.

Non so	dove.
Non sai	quando.
Non sa	come.
Non sappiamo	chi.
Non sapete.	quanto.
Non sanno	quanti.
	quanta.
	quante.
	quale.
	quali.
	che cosa.
	perchè.

I don't	*know*	*where.*
You don't		*when.*
He/she doesn't		*how.*
We don't		*who.*
You don't		*how much* (m .).
They don't		*how many* (m.).
		how much (f.).
		how many (f.).
		which (replacing a sing. noun).
		which (replacing a pl. noun).
		what.
		why.

9.	Che bel quadro!	*What a fine painting!*
	Lo guardi.	*Look at it.*
	Lei lo c*o*mpera, vero?	*You are buying it, aren't you?*
	Lo vende?	*Is he selling it?*
	Lo prenderò se egli lo vende.	*I'll take it if he sells it.*
	Che bella stampa!	*What a fine print!*
	La guardi.	*Look at it.*
	Lei la c*o*mpera, vero?	*You are buying it, aren't you?*
	La prenderò se egli la vende.	*I'll take it if he sells it.*
	Che belle fotogr*a*fie!	*What fine photographs!*
	Le guardi.	*Look at them.*
	Lei le c*o*mpera, vero?	*You are buying them, aren't you?*
	Le prenderò se egli le vende.	*I'll take them if he sells them.*
	Non sono da v*e*ndere.	*They are not for sale.*
	Che peccato!	*What a pity!*

10.	(Io)	aspetto	l'*a*utobus.	*I*	*am waiting for*	*the bus.*
		aspetterò	il treno.		*shall wait for*	*the train.*
	(Tu)	aspetti	il tram.	*You*	*are waiting for*	*the tram.*
		aspetterai	la metropolitana.		*will wait for*	*the Underground.*
	(Egli)	aspetta	i miei amici.	*He*	*is waiting for*	*my friends.*
	(Essa)	aspetterà	qualche minuto.	*She*	*will wait for*	*a few minutes.*
	(Noi)	aspettiamo	qualcuno.	*We*	*are waiting for*	*somebody.*
		aspetteremo	una l*e*ttera.		*will wait for*	*a letter.*
	(Voi)	aspettate	una cartolina.	*You*	*are waiting for*	*a postcard.*
		aspetterete	un telegramma.		*will wait for*	*a telegram.*
	(Essi)	aspettano	un v*a*glia.	*They*	*are waiting for*	*a postal order.*
	(Esse)	aspetteranno	una telefonata.		*will wait for*	*a telephone call.*

1. In the sentence *Io lo vedo* (I see him), *lo* is the direct object. In the sentence *Io gli do un libro* (I give him a book), *gli* is the indirect object, since what I actually give (i.e. the direct object) is *un libro*.

The dative (i.e. indirect object) pronouns—*gli* (to him), *le* (to her, or to you, singular polite form), and *loro* (to them, or to you, plural polite form)—must be distinguished from the accusative (i.e. direct object pronouns) *lo, la, li, le* (see Lesson IV), and also from the articles.

The following table sets out the Nominative, Accusative and Dative forms of the personal pronouns.

	NOMINATIVE (*subject*)	ACCUSATIVE (*direct object*)	DATIVE (*indirect object*)
SINGULAR			
1*st person*	io	mi	mi
2*nd person* (*fam.*)	tu	ti	ti
2*nd person* (*pol.*)	lei	la	le
3*rd person* (*m.*)	egli (*he*), esso (*it*)	lo	gli
3*rd person* (*f.*)	ella (*she*). essa (*she* or *it*)	la	le
PLURAL			
1*st person*	noi	ci	ci
2*nd person* (*fam.*)	voi	vi	vi
2*nd person* (*pol.*)	loro	li (*m.*); le (*f.*)	loro (*m. and f.*)
3*rd person* (*m.*)	essi	li	loro
3*rd person* (*f.*)	esse	le	loro

Both the direct and indirect object pronouns precede the verb, with the exception of *loro*, which follows it.

If, however, the verb is an infinitive, an imperative affirmative,[1] or a present or past participle, the pronouns follow the verb and are joined to it, e.g.

> vederlo, *to see it;* M*a*ngialo! *Eat it!*; vedendolo, *seeing it*; ved*u*tolo, *having seen it*.

[1] but the pronoun precedes the imperative affirmative forms of the 2nd (polite) and 3rd persons singular and plural.

2. The endings of the Imperative in the three conjugations are as follows. An example is also given of those verbs of the third conjugation which add *–isc–* to their stem.

	Verbs ending in –are	*Verbs ending in –ere*	*Verbs ending in –ire*	(*–ire* + *–isc–*)
SINGULAR				
2nd person (*fam.*)	canta	bevi	parti	finisci
2nd person (*pol.*) / *3rd person* (*let him sing, etc.*)	canti	beva	parta	finisca
PLURAL				
1st person (*let us sing, etc.*)	cantiamo	beviamo	partiamo	finiamo
2nd person (*fam.*)	cantate	bevete	partite	finite
2nd person (*pol.*) / *3rd person* (*let them sing, etc.*)	c*a*ntino	b*e*vano	p*a*rtano	fin*i*scano

N.B.—In the Imperative the negative form of the familiar second person singular is like the infinitive, e.g. *non cantare*, do not sing. For the other persons the negative form is obtained by placing *non* in front of the Imperative.

Undicesima Lezione

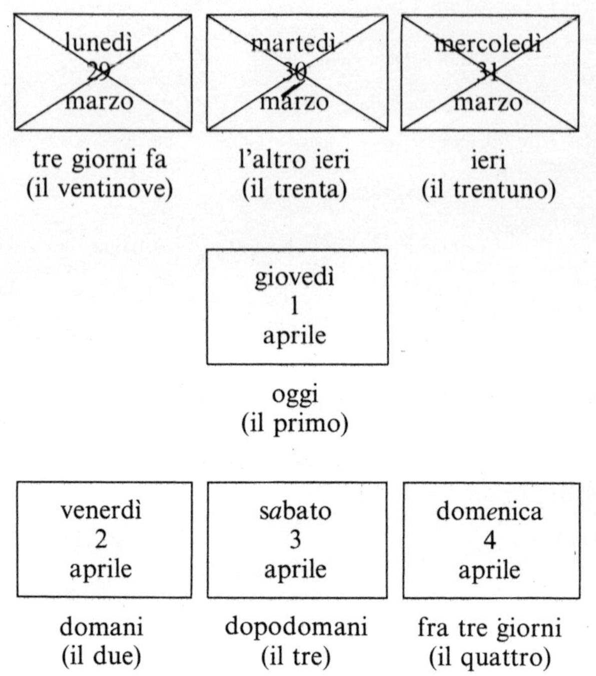

Una Visita

A: *Il Signor Rossi.* B: *La Signora Rossi.* C: *La loro figlia Carla* D: *Walter Brown, un giovane americano.*

(*Nel salotto*[1] *dell'appartamento dei Rossi. Il Signor Rossi legge*[2] *il giornale. La Signora Rossi lavora a maglia.*[3] *Carla scrive*[4] *una lettera. Il campanello suona.*[5])

B (*a sua figlia*): Vuoi andare a vedere chi è?

[1] il salotto, *drawing-room.*
[2] leggere, *to read.*
[3] lavorare a m*a*glia, *to knit.*
[4] scr*i*vere, *to write.*
[5] il campanello suona, *the bell rings.*

(*Carla va alla porta d'entrata e l'apre. È Walter che ha suonato.*)

D: *A*bita[6] qui il Signor Rossi?

C: Sì, venga avanti, prego.

D: Potrei[7] vederlo? Ho una l*e*ttera per lui.

C: Si acc*o*modi.[8] Mi scusi un momento, vado ad avvertire[9] mio padre. (*Entra nel salotto.*)

A: Chi è?

C: È un giovanotto[10] che non conosco. Ti ha portato questa l*e*ttera.

B: Che cosa è?

A (*leggendo*): È una l*e*ttera d'introduzione. Il mio amico Ant*o*nio di Nuova York mi manda[11] un gi*o*vane americano che viene a Roma per studiare m*u*sica. (*Va nell'ingresso.*[12])
Buongiorno, Signor Brown. Gli amici dei miei amici sono anche amici miei. (*Si stringono la mano.*[13]) Non vuole t*o*gliersi[14] il sopr*a*bito?

D: Gr*a*zie. Spero di non disturbare.

A: Niente affatto.[15] È da molto tempo che è a Roma?

D: Sono arrivato l'altroi*e*ri.[16]

A: Andiamo nel salotto. (*Ci vanno.*) Vi presento il Signor Brown. (*A Walter.*) Mia m*o*glie, mia f*i*glia Carla.

B, C: Molto piacere.

D: Molto lieto[17] di fare la loro conoscenza.[18]

A (*offrendogli una sigaretta*): Fuma?

D (*prendendo la sigaretta*): Gr*a*zie.

A: Beve un bicchierino di marsala?[19]

D: Volentieri, gr*a*zie.

[6] abitare, *to dwell.*
[7] potrei, *could I.*
[8] si accomodi, *take a seat.*
[9] avvertire, *to inform.*
[10] il giovanotto, *young man.*
[11] mandare, *to send.*
[12] l'ingresso, *entrance hall.*
[13] str*i*ngersi la mano, *to shake hands.*
[14] togliersi, *to take off.*
[15] niente affatto, *not at all.*
[16] l'altroieri, *the day before yesterday.*
[17] molto lieto, *very pleased.*
[18] la conoscenza, *acquaintance.*
[19] la marsala, *a wine similar to sherry.*

B: Vorrà farci il piacere di cenare con noi questa sera?

D: La ringr*a*zio molto, ma un mio amico ha prenotato[20] dei posti all'*o*pera, e ceneremo pure[21] in città.

B: Pazienza. Verrà[22] un altro giorno, vero?

D: Con molto piacere.

B: Vediamo[23]—oggi è lunedì, domani[24] sera ho degli impegni.[25] Dopodomani verso le sette, se va bene per lei.

D: Va ben*i*ssimo. Verrò con molto piacere.

A (*portando una bottiglia e dei bicchierini*): È marsala dolce. (*Riempie*[26] *i bicchierini.*) Alla sua salute.[27]

D: Alla sua.

[20] prenotare, *to book.*
[21] pure, *also, as well.*
[22] verrà, *you will come.*
[23] vediamo, *let us see.*
[24] domani, *tomorrow.*
[25] gli impegni, *engagements.*
[26] riempire, *to fill.*
[27] alla sua salute, *your health.*

Fluency Practice

1.

(Io) le dico	di venire più tardi.	*I tell you*	*to come later.*
(Egli) mi dice	di farlo adesso.	*He tells me*	*to do it now.*
(Essi) ci d*i*cono	di non farlo.	*They tell us*	*not to do it.*
(Io) gli dico	di non andarci.	*I tell him*	*not to go there.*
(Noi) diciamo loro	che è troppo tardi.	*We tell them*	*that it is too late.*

2. CHE DATA È OGGI? / QUANTI NE ABBIAMO (OGGI)? — WHAT IS TODAY'S DATE?

il primo genn*a*io.	*January* 1*st.*
il due febbr*a*io.	*February* 2*nd.*
l'otto marzo.	*March* 8*th.*
il tr*e*dici aprile.	*April* 13*th.*
il d*o*dici m*a*ggio.	*May* 12*th.*
il quatt*o*rdici giugno.	*June* 14*th.*
il qu*i*ndici l*u*glio.	*July* 15*th.*
il s*e*dici agosto.	*August* 16*th.*
il venti settembre.	*September* 20*th.*
il diciannove ottobre.	*October* 19*th.*
il diciotto novembre.	*November* 18*th.*
il diciassette dicembre.	*December* 17*th.*

3.

Venga a trovarmi	dom*e*nica	primo	genn*a*io	all'una	e cinque.
Noi partiamo	lunedì	due	febbr*a*io	alle due	e un quarto.
Essi arr*i*vano	martedì	tre	marzo	alle tre	e mezzo.
Posso vederla	mercoledì	dieci	aprile	alle quattro	meno dieci.
	giovedì	*u*ndici	m*a*ggio	alle cinque	
	venerdì	venti	giugno	alle sei	
	s*a*bato	ventidue	l*u*glio	alle sette	
			agosto	alle otto	
			settembre	alle nove	
			ottobre	alle dieci	
			novembre	alle *u*ndici	
			dicembre	alle d*o*dici	
				a mezzogiorno.	
				a mezzanotte.	
				al mattino.	
				al pomer*i*ggio.	
				alla sera.	

Come and see me	(*on*)	*Sunday*	*the first*	(*of*)	*January*	*at*	*one*	*five.*
We are leaving		*Monday*	*the second*		*February*		*two*	*fifteen.*
They arrive		*Tuesday*	*the third*		*March*		*three*	*thirty.*
I can see you		*Wednesday*	*the tenth*		*April*		*four*	*less ten.*[1]
		Thursday	*the eleventh*		*May*		*five*	
		Friday	*the twentieth*		*June*		*six*	
		Saturday	*the twenty-second*		*July*		*seven*	
					August		*eight*	
					September		*nine*	
					October		*ten*	
					November		*eleven*	
					December		*twelve*	
							midday.	
							midnight.	
						in the morning.		
						in the afternoon.		
						in the evening.		

[1] i.e., ten to —

4. CHE GIORNO (DELLA SETTIMANA) È OGGI?

Oggi è lunedì.
Domani sarà martedì.
Dopodomani sarà mercoledì.
Giovedì (noi) avremo una lezione d'italiano.
Venerdì andremo a teatro.
Sabato andremo a giocare al tennis.
Dom*e*nica andremo in chiesa.

WHAT DAY OF THE WEEK IS IT?

Today is Monday.
Tomorrow will be Tuesday.
The day after tomorrow will be Wednesday.
On Thursday we shall have an Italian lesson.
On Friday we shall go to the theatre.
We shall go to play tennis on Saturday.
We shall go to church on Sunday.

5.

(Io) resto (Tu) resti (Egli) resta (Noi) restiamo (Voi) restate (Essi) r*e*stano	qui	dalle 7 alle 9. dall'8 al 15 giugno. da s*a*bato 11 a martedì 14.
		fino al 31 m*a*ggio. fino a venerdì pr*o*ssimo. fino alla fine di questo mese. fino al princ*i*pio del mese pr*o*ssimo.
		(per) qu*i*ndici giorni. (per) tre settimane. (per) sei mesi. fino a lunedì mattina. fino a martedì sera.

I am staying *You are staying* *He is staying* *We are staying* *You are staying* *They are staying*	*here*	*from 7 to 9 o'clock.* *from June 8th to 15th.* *from Saturday the 11th until Tuesday the 14th.*
		until May 31st. *until next Friday.* *until the end of this month.* *until the beginning of next month.*
		(for) a fortnight. *(for) three weeks.* *(for) six months.* *until Monday morning.* *until Tuesday evening.*

6. Quando è nato (nata) (lei)?
Sono nato (nata) il ventun marzo.

When were you born?
I was born on March 21st.

Quando è nato suo f*i*glio?
È nato il ventidue giugno.

When was your son born?
He was born on June 22nd.

Quando è nata sua f*i*glia?
È nata il trenta agosto.

When was your daughter born?
She was born on August 30th.

7.

(Io) f*a*ccio	italiano a scuola.	*I*	*do(es) Italian at school.*
(Tu) fai	ginn*a*stica ogni mattina.	*You*[1]	*do(es) exercises each morning.*
(Lei) fa	dello sport.	*You*[2]	*go(es) in for sports.*
(Egli) fa	del tennis.	*He*	*play(s) tennis.*
(Essa) fa	del ciclismo.	*She*	*go(es) in for cycling.*
(Noi) facciamo	dell'automobilismo.	*We*	*go(es) in for motoring.*
(Voi) fate	la c*a*mera.	*You*[3]	*clean(s) the room.*
(Loro) fanno	le valige.	*You*[4]	*do(es) the packing.*
(Essi) fanno	delle provviste.	*They*[5]	*lay(s) in provisions.*
(Esse) fanno	una passeggiata.	*They*[6]	*take(s) a walk.*

8.

(Io)	leggo / scrivo	molti / troppi / pochi / ancora dei (degli) / abbastanza	libri. / romanzi. / saggi / art*i*coli. / rapporti.
(Tu)	leggi / scrivi		
(Lei) (Egli) (Essa)	legge / scrive		
(Noi)	leggiamo / scriviamo	molte / troppe / poche / ancora delle / abbastanza	l*e*ttere. / novelle. / poes*i*e. / st*o*rie. / fiabe.
(Voi)	leggete / scrivete		
(Loro) (Essi) (Esse)	leggono / scr*i*vono		
(Io)	leggerò / scriverò		

I	*read / write*	*many / too many / few / some more / enough*	*books. / novels. / essays. / articles. / reports.*
You[1]			
You[2] *He She*	*read(s) / write(s)*		
We	*read / write*	*many / too many / few / some more / enough*	*letters. / short stories. / poems. / stories. / fairy tales.*
You[3]			
You[4] *They*[5] *They*[6]	*read / write*		
I shall	*read / write*		

[1] familiar singular. [2] polite singular. [3] familiar plural. [4] polite plural. [5] masculine. [6] feminine.

9.	È	il suo	primo secondo terzo	libro d'italiano.	*It is*	*his* *her*	*first* *second* *third*	*Italian book.*

Un biglietto	di	prima seconda	classe.	*A*	*first* *second*	*class ticket.*

Explanations

1. We have seen (Lesson I) that in Italian questions can be formed merely by intonation, without changing the order of words, e.g.

Le hanno scritto una lettera.	*They wrote you a letter.*
Le hanno scritto una lettera?	*Did they write you a letter?*

If, however, a sentence starts with an interrogative adverb, the question is formed by inversion of the subject with the verb, e.g.

Quando partirà suo fratello?	*When will your brother leave?*
Quanto costa questo libro?	*How much does this book cost?*
Dove abita Giovanni?	*Where does John live?*
Che cosa le ha scritto suo zio?	*What did your uncle write to you?*

2. The ordinal numbers from one to ten are *primo, secondo, terzo, quarto, quinto, sesto, settimo, ottavo, nono, decimo.*

From 'eleventh' onwards they are formed from the cardinal numbers, which drop the last vowel and add *–esimo*: *undicesimo, dodicesimo, tredicesimo, ventesimo,* etc.

The date is always expressed with cardinal numbers, except for the first of the month, e.g.

Quanti ne abbiamo?	*What day of the month is it?*
Ne abbiamo qu*i*ndici.	*It is the* 15*th.*
È il primo di giugno.	*It is June* 1*st.*

Names of kings, etc., take the ordinal numbers *without an article,* e.g.

Enrico Quarto, *Henry IV*

Dodicesima Lezione

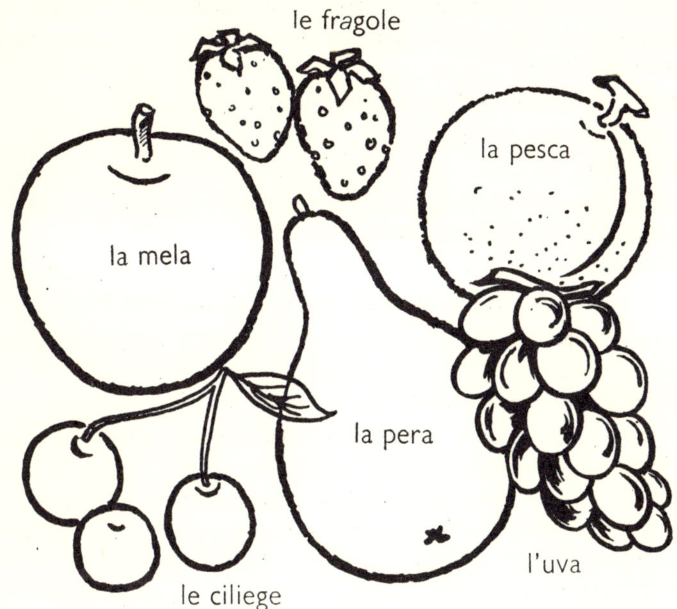

AL MERCATO

A: *La Signora Rossi.* B: *La Signorina Rossi.* C: *La venditrice.*

(*La Signora Rossi e sua figlia vanno al mercato. Il mercato è in due file*[1] *lungo una via ingombra*[2] *di carretti*[3] *e bancarelle.*[4] *Esse si fermano presso una venditrice di verdura.*)

A: Ha dei fagiolini?[5]

C: No, non è ancora la stagione.

A: Ci sono degli asparagi?[6]

[1] la fila, *row.*
[2] ingombro, *encumbered.*
[3] il carretto, *barrow.*
[4] la bancarella, *stand.*
[5] i fagiolini, *French beans.*
[6] gli asparagi, *asparagus.*

C: Sì, ce ne sono. Guardi, signora, come sono belli.

A: Quanto costano al mazzo?[7]

C: 170 lire.

A: Sono cari! Ne prendo un mazzo se me lascia[8] per 150 lire.

C: Impossibile; è quanto costa a me. Glielo lascio a 160 lire perchè[9] lei è una buona cliente.

A: Bene, lo prenderò. Quanto costano le carote, oggi?

C: Quaranta lire al chilo.

A: Me ne dia un chilo.

C: Ecco, signora. Desidera altro?[10] Un bel cavolfiore,[11] signora? Guardi come sono freschi.[12]

A: No, per oggi questo è tutto. Quanto le devo?

C: 160 lire gli asparagi e 40 le carote, fanno duecento lire.

(*La Signora Rossi le dà un biglietto da* 500 *lire, e la venditrice le dà* 300 *lire di resto.*)

C: Grazie tante. Arrivederla signora. Arrivederla signorina.

A (*a sua figlia*): Ed ora comperiamo della frutta. Eccone qui della bella.

(*Esse comperano delle mele e delle ciliege. Poi attraversano*[13] *la via per comperare del burro, del formaggio e delle uova.*[14] *Quando hanno finito gli acquisti*[15] *la loro sporta*[16] *è piena,*[17] *ed esse ritornano a casa.*)

[7] il mazzo, *bunch.*
[8] lasciare, *to leave, to let have.*
[9] perchè, *because.*
[10] altro, (*something*) *else.*
[11] il cavolfiore, *cauliflower.*
[12] fresco, *fresh.*
[13] attraversare, *to cross.*
[14] un uovo, *egg* (*pl.* uova).
[15] un acquisto, *purchase.*
[16] la sporta, *shopping-bag.*
[17] pieno, *full.*

Fluency Practice

1.	Mi dia	il biglietto.	*Give me*	*the ticket.*
	Ci porti	la cartolina.	*Bring us*	*the postcard.*
	Gli mandi	i francobolli.	*Send him*	*the stamps.*
	Le presti	il disco.	*Lend her*	*the record.*
	Venda loro	i giornali.	*Sell them*	*the newspapers.*
	Restituisca loro	le riviste.	*Return them*	*the magazines.*

2.

Me	lo	dia.
Ce	la	porti.
	li	mandi.
	le	venda.
	ne	compri.

Give	*it* (m.)	*to me.*
Bring	*it* (f.)	*to us.*
Send	*them* (m.)	
Sell	*them* (f.)	
Buy	*some*	

Glielo	venda.
Gliela	mandi.
Glieli	porti.
Gliele	dia.
Gliene	compri.

Sell	*it* (m.)	*to him* (*her*).
Send	*it* (f.)	
Bring	*them* (m.)	
Give	*them* (f.)	
Buy	*some*	

Lo	venda	(a) loro.
La	dia	
Li	porti	
Le	restituisca	
Ne	mandi	

Sell	*it* (m.)	*to them.*
Give	*it* (f.)	
Bring	*them* (m.)	
Return	*them* (f.)	
Send	*some*	

3.

Non	me	lo	dia.
	ce	la	porti.
		li	restituisca.
		le	paghi.

Don't	*give*	*it* (m.)	*to me.*
	bring	*it* (f.)	*to us.*
	return	*them* (m.)	
	pay	*them* (f.)	

Non	glielo	porti.
	gliela	venda.
	glieli	dia.
	gliele	paghi

Don't	*bring*	*it* (m.)	*to him* (*her*).
	sell	*it* (f.)	
	give	*them* (m.)	
	pay	*them* (f.)	

Non	lo	porti	(a) loro.
	la	venda	
	li	dia	
	le		

Don't	*bring*	*it* (m.)	*to them.*
	sell	*it* (f.)	
	give	*them* (m.)	
		them (f.)	

4.

Io (non)	glielo	do.
	gliela	mostro.
	glieli	presto.
	gliele	mando.

I am (*not*)	*giving*	*it* (m.)	*to you* (sing.)/*to him*/*her.*
	showing	*it* (f.)	
	lending	*them* (m.)	
	sending	*them* (f.)	

Io (non)	vendo	loro	il biglietto.
	restituisco		la cartolina.
	presto		i francobolli.

I am (*not*)	*selling*	*you* (pl.) (*them*)	*the ticket.*
	returning		*the postcard.*
	lending		*the stamps.*

5.

Egli (non)	me	lo	dà.	*He is* (*not*)	*giving*	*it* (m.)	*to me.*
Essa (non)	ce	la	mostra.	*She is* (*not*)	*showing*	*it* (f.)	*to us.*
		li	vende.		*selling*	*them* (m.)	
		le	paga.		*paying*	*them* (f.)	

Egli (non)	glielo	dà.	*He is* (*not*)	*giving*	*it* (m.)	*to you/him/her.*
Essa (non)	gliela	mostra.	*She is* (*not*)	*showing*	*it* (f.)	
	glieli	vende.		*selling*	*them* (m.)	
	gliele	paga.		*paying*	*them* (f.)	

Egli (non)	dà	loro	il biglietto.	*He is* (*not*)	*giving*	*you* (pl.) (*them*)	*the ticket.*
Essa (non)	mostra		la cartolina.	*She is* (*not*)	*showing*		*the postcard.*
	vende		i francobolli.		*selling*		*the stamps.*
	paga				*paying*		

6.

Essi (non)	me lo	danno.	*They are* (*not*)	*giving it* (m.)	*to me.*
Esse (non)	ce la	m*o*strano.	*They are* (*not*)	*showing it* (f.)	*to us.*
	glieli	pr*e*stano.		*lending them* (m.)	*to him/her.*
	gliele	restitu*i*scono.		*returning them* (f.)	*to him/her.*

Essi (non)	lo	danno	(a) loro.	*They are* (*not*)	*giving*	*it* (m.)	*to you* (pl.) (*them*)
Esse (non)	la	m*o*strano			*showing*	*it* (f.)	
	li	pr*e*stano			*lending*	*them* (m.)	
	le	restitu*i*scono			*returning*	*them* (f.)	

7.

Perchè	non	me lo	dà?	*Why*	*don't you*	*give*	*it* (m.)	*to me?*
		ce la	vende?			*sell*	*it* (f.)	*to us?*
		glieli	mostra?			*show*	*them* (m.)	*to him/her?*
		gliele	porta?			*bring*	*them* (f.)	

Perchè	non	lo	dà	(a) loro?	*Why*	*don't you*	*give*	*it* (m.)	*to them?*
		la	vende				*sell*	*it* (f.)	
		li	mostra				*show*	*them* (m.)	
		le	porta				*bring*	*them* (f.)	

8.	Di*a*moglielo.	*Let us*	*give it* (m.)	*to him/her*
	Paghi*a*mogliela.		*pay it* (f.)	
	Vendi*a*moglieli.		*sell them* (m.)	
	Mostri*a*mogliele.		*show them* (f.)	
	Di*a*molo loro.	*Let us*	*give it* (m.)	*to them.*
	Paghi*a*mola loro.		*pay it* (f.)	
	Vendi*a*moli loro.		*sell them* (m.)	
	Mostri*a*mole loro.		*show them* (f.)	

9.	Me ne darà.	*He* (*she*) *will give me some.*
	Gliene porterà.	*He* (*she*) *will bring you* (*him, her*) *some.*
	Gliene manderemo.	*We'll send him* (*her, you*) *some.*
	Non prest*a*tegliene.	*Don't lend him* (*her*) *any.*

Explanations

1. The object pronoun *loro* always follows the verb (see page 62).

2. When *mi, ti, si, ci* and *vi* precede *ne* or the pronouns *lo, la, li* and *le*, the *–i* changes into *–e* to give the forms *me, te, se, ce, ve,* e.g.

Mi dia il biglietto.	*Give me the ticket.*
Me lo dia.	*Give it to me.*

gli and *le* both become *glie* and fuse into one word with the pronoun that follows:

Gli do un libro.	*I give him a book.*
Le mando una cartolina.	*I send you/her a card.*
Glielo, gliela do.	*I give it to you* (*or to him/her*).
Glieli, gliele do.	*I give them to you* (*or to him/her.*)
Gliene do.	*I give some to you* (*or to him/her*).
Gliene dia.	*Give him/her some.*

3. When there are two object pronouns the *indirect* precedes the *direct* (contrary to English usage), i.e. any in the first column may be combined with any one in the second, e.g.

me	*lo*
glie-	*la*
ce	*li*
ve	*le*
	ne

Tredicesima Lezione

Una signora ha dimenticato l'ombrello.

Un signore ha perso il portafoglio.

Hanno vuotato tutte le bott*i*glie.
(Hanno bevuto dello spumante.)

Hanno finito il pasto.
(Hanno mangiato bene.)

Preparativi per il Pranzo

A: *Il Signor Rossi.* B: *La Signora Rossi.* C: *Carla.* D: *Walter.*

(La Signora Rossi entra nella sala da pranzo, dove Carla sta preparando la tavola.)

B: Hai finito,[1] Carla?

C: Non del tutto.[2] Dove metto questo?

B: Che cosa è?

C: Il cestino[3] del pane.

B: Mettilo[4] sulla credenza,[5] per ora. Dove hai messo la saliera?[6]

C: È sulla tavola.

B: Vediamo. No, Carla, non così.[7] Il coltello[8] a destra, e la forchetta[9] a sinistra.

C: Così, mamma?

B: Sì, così va bene. Hai portato i bicchieri?

C: Li ho messi sulla credenza.

B: Li metto io sulla tavola. Tu puoi portare la minestra. Io vado a chiamare[10] gli altri. (*Mette i bicchieri sulla tavola, e poi va nel salotto.*) Il pranzo è pronto. Volete accomodarvi? (*Vanno nella sala da pranzo.*) (*A Walter.*) Si sieda qui, a fianco[11] di mia figlia.

A: Ha già visitato i musei del Vaticano?

D: Non ancora.[12] Ieri ho visitato il Colosseo e quest'oggi andrò alla Villa Borghese.

(Carla arriva con la minestra.)

A: Ah, ecco la minestra!

(La Signora Rossi serve la minestra.)

C: Buon appetito a tutti.

A, B, D *(assieme)*: Buon appetito!

[1] finire, *to finish.*
[2] non del tutto, *not completely.*
[3] il cestino, *basket.*
[4] mettere, *to put* (mettilo, *put it*).
[5] la credenza, *sideboard.*
[6] la saliera, *cruet.*
[7] così, *so, like that.*
[8] il coltello, *knife.*
[9] la forchetta, *fork.*
[10] chiamare, *to call.*
[11] a fianco, *at the side, next to.*
[12] non ancora, *not yet.*

Fluency Practice

1.

Ha	mangiato?	*Have you*[1] (pol. sing.)	*eaten ?*
	giocato?	*Has he/she*	*played ?*
	dormito bene?		*slept well ?*
	chiesto il conto?		*asked for the bill ?*
	perso qualche cosa?		*lost anything ?*

2.

Non ha	bevuto il latte?	*Haven't you*[2] (pol. sing.)	*drunk your/his/her milk ?*
	fatto il bagno?	*Hasn't he/she*	*taken your/his/her bath ?*
	scritto una lettera?		*written a letter ?*
	fatto una passeggiata?		*taken a walk?*
	detto questo?		*said this ?*
	finito questo libro?		*finished this book ?*

3.

(Io) ho	mangiato.	*I have*[3]	*eaten.*
(Io) non ho	dormito bene.	*I have not*	*slept well.*
(Egli) ha	finito il lavoro.	*He has*	*finished the work.*
(Egli) non ha	restituito il libro.	*He has not*	*returned the book.*
(Essi) hanno	venduto la casa.	*They have*	*sold the house.*
(Essi) non hanno	avuto un incidente.	*They have not*	*had an accident.*
(Noi) abbiamo	imparato l'italiano.	*We have*	*learned Italian.*
(Noi) non abbiamo	capito questo.	*We have not*	*understood this.*

4.

L'ha sentito (sentita) lei?	*Have you heard*	*it ?*
L'ha pagato (pagata) lei?	*Have you/has she/paid*	*him ?*
L'ha accompagnato (accompagnata) lui?	*Has he accompanied*	*her ?*
L'hanno visto (vista) loro?	*Have you* (pl.) or *have they seen*	

[1] or *did you eat, play,* etc.
[2] or *didn't you drink, take,* etc.
[3] or *I ate, slept,* etc.

5.	Li ho venduti io?	*Have I sold*	*them* (m.)?
	Li ha finiti lei?	*Have you/has she/finished*	
	Li ha comperati lui?	*Has he bought*	
	Li hanno presi loro?	*Have you* (pl.) or *have they taken*	

6.	Le ho vendute io?	*Have I sold*	*them* (f.)?
	Le ha finite lei?	*Have you/has she/finished*	
	Le ha comperate lui?	*Has he bought*	
	Le hanno prese loro?	*Have you* (pl.) or *have they taken*	

7.	(Io) l'ho trovato (trovata).	*I have*	*found*	*it.*
	(Io) non l'ho cercato (cercata).	*I haven't*	*looked for*	*her.*
	(Egli) l'ha visto (vista).	*He has*	*seen*	*him.*
	(Essa) non l'ha aspettato (aspettata).	*She has not*	*waited for*	
	(Essi) l'hanno aiutato (aiutata).	*They* (m.) *have*	*helped*	
	(Essi) non l'hanno chiesto (chiesta).	*They* (m.) *haven't*	*asked for*	
	(Esse) l'hanno perso (persa).	*They* (f.) *have*	*lost*	

8.	(Io) li (le) ho comperati (comperate).	*I have*	*bought*	*them.*
	(Io) non li (le) ho venduti (vendute).	*I haven't*	*sold*	
	(Egli) li (le) ha invitati (invitate).	*He has*	*invited*	
	(Essa) non li (le) ha aspettati (aspettate).	*She hasn't*	*waited for*	
	(Essi) li (le) hanno letti (lette).	*They* (m.) *have*	*read*	
	(Esse) non li (le) hanno dimenticati (dimenticate).	*They* (f.) *haven't*	*forgotten*	

9.	Gli	ha	parlato?	*Did*	*you*	*speak to*	*him?*
	Le		scritto?			*write to*	*her?*
			riposto?			*answer*	
			chiesto?			*ask*	

Ha	parlato	(a) loro?	*Did*	*you*	*speak to*	*them* (m. and f.)?
	scritto				*write to*	
	risposto				*answer*	
	chiesto				*ask*	

10. Gli / Le | ho | parlato. / scritto. / risposto. — *I* | *spoke to* / *wrote to* / *answered* | *him.* / *her.*

Ho | parlato / scritto / chiesto | (a) loro. — *I* | *spoke to* / *wrote to* / *asked* | *them* (m. and f.)

11. Dov'è stato(a)?	*Where have you been?*
Sono stato(a) alla biblioteca.	*I have been to the library.*
Che cosa ha fatto ieri?	*What did you do yesterday?*
Ho risposto ad alcune l*e*ttere.	*I replied to some letters.*
Ha scritto molte l*e*ttere?	*Did you write many letters?*
Ne ho scritte una dozzina.	*I wrote about a dozen (of them).*
Ha pranzato bene?	*Did you have a good dinner?*
Ho pranzato ben*i*ssimo.	*I had an excellent dinner.*
Innanzitutto un'insalata di pomodori, poi una cotoletta d'agnello, seguita da fagiolini.	*First a tomato salad, then a lamb chop, followed by French beans.*
Come dolce una torta di mele.	*As a sweet an apple tart.*
Per la cena ho comperato del pane, un etto[1] di prosciutto, delle pesche, e una bott*i*glia di birra.	*For supper I bought some bread, a quarter pound of ham, peaches, and a bottle of beer.*
Dove ha comperato tutte queste cose?	*Where did you buy all that?*
I panini? Li ho comperati dal panettiere di fronte all'albergo.	*The rolls? I bought them at the baker's opposite the hotel.*
Il prosciutto? L'ho comperato alla salumer*i*a in fondo alla via.	*The ham? I bought it at the pork butcher's at the end of the street.*
La birra alla bottiglier*i*a all'*a*ngolo, e le pesche nel mercato della piazza principale.	*The beer at the wine-shop at the corner and the peaches in the market in the main square.*

[1] a hectogram, about ¼ lb.

Explanations

1. The Perfect Tense, or *Passato Prossimo*, is formed in Italian in the same way as in English, that is, by the Present Tense of *avere* (to have)[1] followed by a Past Participle.

The endings of the Past Participle are:

–ato	for verbs	ending	in	*–are*
–uto	,,	,,	,,	*–ere*
–ito	,,	,,	,,	*–ire*

The following verbs, amongst others, are irregular:

INFINITIVE	PAST PARTICIPLE	INFINITIVE	PAST PARTICIPLE
*e*ssere	stato	scr*i*vere	scritto
avere	avuto	l*e*ggere	letto
m*e*ttere	messo	vedere	visto (*also* veduto)
dire	detto	p*e*rdere	perso (*also* perduto)
chi*e*dere	chiesto	fare	fatto

2. The *Passato Prossimo* not only expresses what has just happened, but also what happened in the near past. *Ha . . . ?* followed by the past participle, therefore, is the usual translation not only for 'Have you . . .?' but also for 'Did you . . .?'

3. When using *avere* as an auxiliary verb, the past participle of the main verb may or may not agree in gender and number with the direct object:

(*a*) the past participle remains unchanged if it precedes the direct object, e.g. *Ho incontrato le signorine Rossi*;

(*b*) it optionally agrees with the direct object when this precedes it, e.g. *Le signorine che ho incontrato* or *incontrate*;

BUT

(*c*) if the past participle is preceded by a direct object PRONOUN, it must agree with it, e.g. *Le ho incontrate.*

[1] But see next lesson (XIV) for verbs requiring *essere.*

Quattordicesima Lezione

Il Signor Rossi esce.

Il Signor Rossi è uscito.

Sale sull'*a*utobus.

È salito sull'*a*utobus.

Scende.

È caduto.

A: *Il Signor Rossi.* B: *La Signora Rossi.* C: *Carla.* D: *Walter.* E: *Enrico.*

B: Ancora un po' d'insalata?[1]

D: Volentieri. È eccellente.

A: Come trova[2] il mio Chianti?

D: È veramente[3] molto buono.

C: È già stato[4] a teatro, qui a Roma?

D: Sono stato all'*o*pera.

C: Che cosa ha visto?

D: *Il Mefistofele.*

B: Come l'ha trovato?

D: Magn*i*fico. Purtroppo[5] sono arrivato in ritardo,[6] e ho perso[7] il Pr*o*logo.

B: È un peccato. Se vuole le faremo sentire il nostro disco[8] del Pr*o*logo al *Mefistofele.*

D: Gr*a*zie, mi farebbe piacere sentirlo.

B (*a Carla*): Vuoi t*o*gliere i piatti,[9] e portare il dolce?

A: Che cosa abbiamo per dolce?

B: Delle fr*a*gole[10] con panna montata.[11]

(*Carla arriva con il dolce.*)

C: *E*ccolo! (*Carla serve tutti eccetto Enrico.*) Tu hai avuto la tua porzione. È lui che ha montato la panna. Ne ha mangiata la metà, il ghiottone.[12]

D: Lo capisco bene: l'ha trovata irresist*i*bile—ed è davvero deliziosa.[13] Sia buona, lo perdoni.[14]

[1] l'insalata, *salad.*
[2] trovare, *to find.*
[3] veramente, *truly, really.*
[4] stato, *been.*
[5] purtroppo, *unfortunately.*
[6] in ritardo, *late.*
[7] perdere, *to lose, to miss.*
[8] il disco, *record.*
[9] il piatto, *plate.*
[10] la fr*a*gola, *strawberry.*
[11] la panna montata, *whipped cream.*
[12] il ghiottone, *greedy person.*
[13] deliziosa, *delicious.*
[14] lo perdoni, *forgive him.*

B: *E*ccotene,[15] goloso.[16] Ma solo[17] pr*o*prio[18] per far piacere[19] al Signor Walter.

[15] eccotene, *here is some for you.*
[16] goloso, *glutton.*
[17] solo, *only.*
[18] proprio, *indeed.*
[19] far piacere, *to please.*

Fluency Practice

1.

È	uscito (uscita) ieri?
	andato (andata) a teatro?
	arrivato (arrivata) questa mattina?
	partito (partita) ieri sera?

Did you (sing.)	*go out yesterday?*
(also: *Did he/she*)	*go to the theatre?*
	arrive in the morning?
	leave last night?

2.

Io sono	andato (andata)	*I have*	*gone*
Io non sono	uscito (uscita)	*I haven't*	*gone out*
Non sono (io)	arrivato (arrivata)	*Haven't I*	*arrived*
Tu sei	partito (partita)	*You* (fam.) *have*	*left*

Egli (essa) è	salito (salita)	*He/she has*	*gone up*
Egli (essa) non è	sceso (scesa)	*He/she hasn't*	*gone down*
Non è (egli/essa)	caduto (caduta)	*Hasn't he/she*	*fallen*

3.

Noi siamo	andati (andate)	*We have*	*gone*
Noi non siamo	usciti (uscite)	*We haven't*	*gone out*
Non siamo (noi)	arrivati (arrivate)	*Haven't we*	*arrived*
Loro sono	partiti (partite)	*You* (pl.) *have*	*left*
Sono (loro)	saliti (salite)	*Have you* (pl.)	*gone up*
Non sono (loro)	scesi (scese)	*Haven't you* (pl.)	*gone down*
Essi (esse) sono	caduti (cadute)	*They have*	*fallen*
Sono (essi/esse)	stati (state)	*Have they*	*been*
Non sono (essi/esse)	venuti (venute)	*Haven't they*	*come*

4.

C'è	andato (andata)?
	salito (salita)?
	sceso (scesa)?
	arrivato (arrivata)?
	venuto (venuta)?

Did you	*go*	*there?*
(*Did he/she*)	*go up*	
	go down	
	arrive	
	come	

5.

Ci	vado.
	salgo.
	scendo.
	arrivo.

I am	*going*	*there.*
	going up	
	going down	
	arriving	

6.

Ci sono	andato (andata).
	salito (salita).
	sceso (scesa).
	arrivato (arrivata).

I	*went*	*there.*
	went up	
	went down	
	arrived	

Ci	andavo	spesso.
	salivo	tutti i giorni.
	scendevo	ogni anno.

I used	*to go*	*there*	*often.*
	to go up		*every day.*
	to go down		*each year.*

7.

Ci	vada!
	entri!
	salga!
	resti!

Go	*there!*
Go in	
Go up	
Stay	

Non ci	vada!
	entri!
	salga!
	resti!

Don't	*go there.*
	go in there.
	go up there.
	stay there.

8.

Sono andato (–a)	dal	panettiere	all'*a*ngolo.
Se ne può avere		macell*a*io	a cento metri da qui.
Lo può comperare		salumiere	all'altra estremità della via.
Li ho comperati		droghiere	vicino alla chiesa.
Le ho comperate		fruttiv*e*ndolo	di fronte.
Lo comprerò		farmacista	nella piazza.
(Io) andavo		pesciv*e*ndolo	dietro alla stazione.
(Io) andrei		tabacc*a*io	davanti al Municipio.
I went to	*the*	*baker's*	*at the corner.*
One can have some at		*butcher's*	*one hundred metres from here.*
You can buy it at		*pork butcher's*	*at the other end of the street.*
I bought them (m.) *at*		*grocer's*	*near the church.*
I bought them (f.) *at*		*greengrocer's*	*opposite.*
I shall buy it at		*chemist's*	*in the square.*
I used to go to		*fishmonger's*	*behind the station.*
I should go to		*tobacconist's*	*in front of the Town Hall.*

9.

DA IMPARARE A MEMORIA	LEARN BY HEART
Che cosa è?	*What is it?*
Che cosa è questo?	*What is this?*
Non è nulla.	*It is nothing.*
Che cosa è quell'edif*i*cio?	*What is that building?*
È l'uff*i*cio postale.	*It is the post-office.*
Va bene.	*It is right.* (*That is right*).
È vero, non trova?	*It is true, isn't it?*
Credo di sì.	*I think so.*
Credo di no.	*I don't think so.*
Ne sono sicuro.	*I am sure of it.*
Non ne sono affatto sicuro.	*I am not at all sure of it.*

1. Verbs denoting motion from one place to another form their compound tenses with e*ssere* (to be). '*È...?*' therefore is the usual translation of 'have you...?' or 'did you...?' in connection with the past participles of *andare, venire, partire, arrivare, entrare, uscire, scendere, salire, cadere,* etc.

Correre (to run) is conjugated with either e*ssere* or *avere*. Verbs which merely indicate a bodily activity are conjugated with *avere,* e.g. *camminare* (to walk), *marciare* (to march), *saltare* (to jump).

When the auxiliary verb e*ssere* is used in the formation of compound tenses, the past participle of the main verb must agree with the subject, e.g. *Enrico è uscito; Carla è entrata.*

2. Descriptions, and habitual and repeated actions in the past, are expressed by the *Imperfetto*. It is also used to express that something was in progress when something else started.

The endings of the *Imperfetto* are as follows for all verbs excepting e*ssere*:

io cantavo	io vendevo	io dormivo
tu cantavi	tu vendevi	tu dormivi
egli cantava	egli vendeva	egli dormiva
noi cantavamo	noi vendevamo	noi dormivamo
voi cantavate	voi vendevate	voi dormivate
essi cant*a*vano	essi vend*e*vano	essi dorm*i*vano

The *Imperfetto* of e*ssere* is:
ero, eri, era, eravamo, eravate, *e*rano.

3. For the *Condizionale* (I should sing, etc.) the endings are as follows:

io canter*e*i	io vender*e*i	io dormir*e*i
tu canteresti	tu venderesti	tu dormiresti
egli canterebbe	egli venderebbe	egli dormirebbe
noi canteremmo	noi venderemmo	noi dormiremmo
voi cantereste	voi vendereste	voi dormireste
essi canter*e*bbero	essi vender*e*bbero	essi dormir*e*bbero

The *Condizionale* of e*ssere* is:
sar*e*i, saresti, sarebbe, saremmo, sareste, sar*e*bbero.

Quindicesima Lezione

(Egli) dorme.

Si sveglia.

Si alza.

Si veste.

AL MATTINO

A: *Il Signor Rossi.* B: *La Signora Rossi.* C: *Carla.* D: *Enrico.*

(*Sono le sette del mattino. La Signora Rossi si alza.* Il Signor Rossi si sveglia.* Carla ed Enrico dormono ancora.*)

B: Hai dormito bene?

A: Sì, grazie, e tu?

B: Non troppo bene. La radio dei vicini[1] mi ha tenuta[2] sveglia fino all'una.

A: Parlerò alla portinaia.[3] Adesso mi faccio la barba.[4]

[1] i vicini, *neighbours.*
[2] tenere, *to keep.*
[3] la portinaia, *doorkeeper.*
[4] farsi la barba, *to shave.*

B (*battendo alle porte delle camere di Carla e di Enrico*): Alz*a*tevi, sono le sette!

(*Carla si alza immediatamente, ma Enrico rimane a letto. Qualche minuto dopo, sua sorella viene nella sua camera.*)

C: Come! Non ti sei ancora alzato? *A*lzati s*u*bito!

D: L*a*sciami dormire ancora cinque minuti. Ho tanto sonno.[5] Non posso alzarmi.

C: Non cercare[6] delle scuse; è ora di alzarsi. Ti alzi, sì o no? Conto fino a tre: uno, due, tre! (*Gli toglie*[7] *le coperte.*[8])

D: L*a*sciami in pace![9]

C: Non dimenticare di lavarti il collo,[10] come al s*o*lito.[11]

(*Enrico le tira*[12] *un cuscino*[13] *senza colpirla.*[14] *Lo raccoglie,*[15] *e si precipita*[16] *nella stanza da bagno, dove suo padre si sta radendo.*[17])

[5] aver sonno, *to be sleepy.*
[6] non cercare, *do not look for* (*negative form of imperative mood, 2nd person sing.*).
[7] togliere, *take out, take away.*
[8] la coperta, *blanket.*
[9] la pace, *peace.*
[10] il collo, *neck.*
[11] come al solito, *as usual.*
[12] tirare, *to throw.*
[13] il cuscino, *pillow.*
[14] colpire, *to hit.*
[15] raccogliere, *to pick up.*
[16] precipitarsi, *to rush.*
[17] radersi, *to shave.*

Fluency Practice

1. Si alzi! — *Get up!*
   Si svegli! — *Wake up!*
   Si acc*o*modi! — *Make yourself comfortable (sit down)!*
   Si diverta! — *Enjoy yourself (have a good time)!*

   Non si bruci! — *Don't burn yourself!*
   Non si tagli! — *Don't cut yourself!*
   Non si alzi! — *Don't get up!*

2. Io mi alzo. / lavo. / vesto. / corico. — *I am getting up. / washing. / getting dressed. / going to bed.*

   Lei si / Egli si / Essa si alza. / lava. / veste. / corica. — *You are / He is / She is getting up. / washing. / dressing. / going to bed.*

Noi ci	vestiamo.	*We are*	*getting dressed.*
	svestiamo.		*getting undressed.*
	corichiamo.		*going to bed.*

Loro si	*a*lzano presto.	*You are*	*getting up early.*
Essi si	c*o*ricano tardi.	*They are*	*going to bed late.*
Esse si	l*a*vano le mani.		*washing their hands.*

3\. Io non mi alzo. — *I am not getting up.*
Lei non si c*o*rica. — *You are not going to bed.*

Egli	non si	veste.	*He*	*is not*	*getting dressed.*
Essa		sveste.	*She*		*getting undressed.*

Noi non ci svestiamo. — *We are not getting undressed.*

Loro	non si	sv*e*gliano.	*You*	*are not*	*waking up.*
Essi		*a*lzano.	*They*		*getting up.*
Esse		v*e*stono.			*getting dressed.*

4\.

Essi	non si	sb*a*gliano	mai.	*They*	*never*	*make a mistake.*
Esse		l*a*vano				*wash.*
		div*e*rtono				*enjoy themselves.*

5\.

Venga con	me.	*Come with*	*me.*
Non vada senza di	lui.	*Don't go without*	*him.*
Non è per	lei.	*It is not for*	*you* (sing.) /*her.*
Appartiene a	noi.	*It belongs to*	*us.*
Non appartiene a	loro.	*It doesn't belong to*	*you* (pl.)/*them.*

6\.

V*e*ngano[1]	da	me	*Come*[1] *to*	*my*	*place*
Non c'è nessuno		noi	*There is no one at*	*our*	
C'è qualcuno		lui	*Is there anyone at*	*his*	
P*a*ssino[1]		lei	*Call at*	*her*	
Non p*a*ssino		loro	*Do not call at*	*their*	

7\.

V*e*ngano	a casa mia	*Come*[2] *to*	*my house*
Non c'è nessuno	a casa nostra	*There is no one at*	*our house*
C'è qualcuno	a casa sua	*Is there anyone at*	*his/her house*
P*a*ssino	a casa loro	*Call at*	*their house*

8\. CHI È? — WHO IS IT?

È	lei.	*It is*	*you.*
	lui.		*he.*
	lei.		*she.*

Sono	io.	*It is*	*I.*
	loro.		*they.*

[1] Imperative, 2nd person plural (polite).

[2] also 'let them come'.

9. Come si chiama?	*What is your/his/her/name?*
Mi chiamo Alberto.	*My name is Albert.*
Come si chiama suo fratello?	*What is your brother's name?*
Si chiama Giuseppe.	*His name is Joseph.*
E sua sorella, come si chiama?	*And what is your sister's name?*
Si chiama Maria.	*Her name is Maria.*

EXPLANATIONS

1. Note the following carefully:

(*a*) *lavare* = to wash, in the sense of 'to do some washing' or 'to wash somebody', e.g.

Maria lava sua sorella.	*Mary washes her sister.*
Giovanni lava l'automobile.	*John washes the car.*

(*b*) *lavarsi* = to wash oneself.

A verb where the same person is both the subject and the object of the action is called a 'reflexive verb'.

2. The reflexive pronouns are:

mi, *myself.*
ti, *yourself* (*familiar form*).
si, *yourself* (*polite form*), *himself, herself, itself, oneself.*
ci, *ourselves.*
vi, *yourselves* (*familiar form*).
si, *yourselves* (*polite form*), *themselves.*

Note from the examples given in the Fluency Practice section that some verbs are reflexive in Italian which are not so in English.

Some of the commonest are: *alzarsi,* to get up; *coricarsi,* to lie down, to go to bed; *prepararsi,* to get ready; *vestirsi,* to get dressed.

3. *Egli, essa, essi, esse* can be used only in connection with verbs. The following pronouns are used independently of verbs, chiefly after prepositions:

lui, *he, him*
lei, *she, her*
loro, *they, them*

For emphasis these pronouns are also used with verbs, e.g. *I Bianchi vanno in vacanza: lui va a Roma, e lei va a Napoli.*

The Bianchis go on holiday: he goes to Rome and she goes to Naples.

Sedicesima Lezione

Fa bel tempo (Fa bello).
(Essa fa un bagno di sole.)

Fa caldo.
(Il signore si asciuga la fronte.)

N*e*vica.
(I bambini si b*u*ttano le palle di neve.)

Piove.
(Il signore apre l'ombrello.)

Tira vento.
(Il vento le porta via il cappello. Essa corre ad afferrarlo.)

Fa freddo.
(La bambina si frega le mani.)

Un Appuntamento[1]

W: *Walter.* C: *Carla.*

(*Walter è nella sua camera. Si è alzato presto*[2] *e ha già fatto colazione. Dopo aver*[3] *trovato il numero dei Rossi sulla guida*[4] *del telefono si avvicina all'apparecchio, stacca*[5] *il ricevitore*[6] *e fa il numero.*)

W: Pronto! Posso parlare con la signorina Carla?
C: Sono io. Chi parla?
W: Sono Walter. Buongiorno signorina, come sta?
C: Molto bene, gr*a*zie, e lei?
W: Non troppo bene: mi sento[7] solo.[8]
C: Oh, p*o*vero Walter! Venga a farci v*i*sita.
W: Verrei volentieri,[9] ma è una giornata cosi bella.[10] Sarebbe m*e*glio passeggiare[11] all'*a*ria aperta. Non vuole fare una passeggiata?
C: Sono così occupata! Devo studiare. Alle *u*ndici ho una lezione d'inglese.
W: Bene. Parleremo solo inglese. Le sarà più *u*tile[12] che studiare.
C: Ma lei, non è venuto a Roma per imparare l'italiano?
W: È vero. Potremo parlare in inglese la metà[13] del tempo, e poi in italiano.
C: È un'*o*ttima idea!
W: Mi sono alzato presto per telefonarle prima della sua lezione. Non può rimandarla?[14]
C: È troppo tardi. Il mio insegnante[15] è già per via.[16] Ma sono l*i*bera nel pomer*i*ggio. Venga a pr*e*ndermi alle tre. Se non le

[1] un appuntamento, *a 'date'.*
[2] presto, *early.*
[3] dopo aver, *after having.*
[4] la guida, *directory.*
[5] staccare, *to unhook.*
[6] il ricevitore, *receiver.*
[7] sentire, *to feel.*
[8] solo, *alone, lonely.*
[9] verrei volentieri, *I should like to.*
[10] è una giornata così bella, *it is such a fine day.*
[11] passeggiare, *to take a walk.*
[12] utile, *useful.*
[13] la metà, *half.*
[14] rimandare, *to postpone.*
[15] l'insegnante, *teacher.*
[16] per via, *on the way.*

dispiace domanderò a mia madre di venire con noi: non si è sentita molto bene questa mattina, e un po' d'*a*ria fresca le farà bene.

W: D'accordo. Verrò alle tre in punto.[17] Arrivederci. (*Posa il ricevitore.*) Sempre sfortunato![18]

[17] in punto, *punctually; 'on the dot'.* [18] sempre sfortunato! *Always unlucky!*

Fluency Practice

1.

Mi sono	lavato.	*I* (m.) *washed myself.*
	lavata.	*I* (f.) *washed myself.*
	vestito(a).	*I dressed myself.*
	alzato(a).	*I got up.*
	coricato(a).	*I went to bed.*

2.

Egli si è	alzato	*He has*	*got up*
Egli non si è	vestito	*He hasn't*	*dressed*
Non si è	svestito	*Hasn't he*	*undressed*
	tagliato		*cut himself*
	bruciato		*burnt himself*
Essa si è	alzata	*She has*	*got up*
Essa non si è	vestita	*She hasn't*	*dressed*
Non si è	riposata	*Hasn't she*	*had a rest*
	coricata		*lain down*
	bruciata		*burnt herself*

3.

Si è alzato.	*He got up.*
Si è vestita.	*She got dressed.*
Non si è riposato?	*Hasn't he had a rest?*
Non si è coricata?	*Hasn't she gone to bed?*

4.

Noi ci siamo svegliati.	*We* (m.) *have woken up.*
Siamo pronte?	*Are we* (f.) *ready?*
Noi non ci siamo vestiti.	*We* (m.) *haven't dressed ourselves.*
Non ci siamo sbagliate?	*Aren't we mistaken?* (f.)

5.

Loro si sono bruciati(e).	*You have burnt yourselves.*
Si sono tagliati(e)?	*Have you cut yourselves?*
Loro non si sono riposati(e).	*You haven't had a rest.*
Non si sono coricati(e)?	*Haven't you gone to bed?*

6.	Essi(e) si sono Si sono Essi(e) non si sono Non si sono	alzati(e) presto vestiti(e) in fretta svestiti(e) sulla spi*a*ggia divertiti(e) molto riposati(e) abbastanza

They have *Have they* *They haven't* *Haven't they*	*got up early* *dressed quickly* *undressed on the beach* *enjoyed themselves a lot* *had sufficient rest*

7.	Mi sono	raffreddato(a). tagliato(a) un dito. bruciato(a) la l*i*ngua. slogato(a) la cav*i*glia. fatto(a) male alla gamba.	*I*	*caught a cold.* *cut my finger.* *burned my tongue.* *sprained an ankle.* *hurt my leg.*

8. Che cos'ha? — *What is the matter with you/him/her?*
Che cos'hanno? — *What is the matter with you* (pl.) */them?*
Si è fatto male? — *Have you/has he/hurt yourself/himself?*
Si è fatta male? — *Have you/has she/hurt yourself/herself?*

9. Dove ha male? — *Where does it hurt?*

Ho male	alla gola. ai denti. alla testa. allo st*o*maco. alla gamba. al piede. al dito. all'*o*cchio. all'or*e*cchio. al gin*o*cchio.	*I have*	*a sore throat.* *toothache.* *a headache.* *a stomach ache.* *a sore leg.* *a sore foot.* *a sore finger.* *a sore eye.* *a sore ear.* *a bad knee.*

10. A che ora si è alzato(a) questa mattina? — *What time did you get up this morning?*
Non è andato(a) a letto tardi ieri? — *Didn't you go to bed late yesterday?*
Dov'è andato(a)? — *Where did you go?*
Non è andato(a) a teatro? — *Didn't you go to the theatre?*
Che cosa ha visto? — *What did you see?*
Ha trovato un buon posto? — *Did you find a good seat?*
Si è divertito(a)? — *Did you enjoy yourself?*

Explanations

1. Reflexive verbs (see Lesson XV) form their *Passato Prossimo* with *essere* (therefore the past participle must agree in gender and number with the subject). '*Si è...?*', therefore, is the usual translation for 'did you...?' or 'have you...?' in connection with reflexive verbs.

2. Note the Present Tense of the verbs *dormire* (to sleep), *servire* (to serve), *sentire* (to feel, to hear):

io	dormo	tu	dormi	lei	dorme
	servo		servi	egli	serve
	sento		senti	essa	sente
noi	dormiamo	voi	dormite	loro	dormono
	serviamo		servite	essi	servono
	sentiamo		sentite	esse	sentono

Reflexive verbs derived from the above are *addormentarsi* (to fall asleep), *servirsi* (to help oneself), *sentirsi* (to feel [well, ill, tired, etc.]).

The *Passato Prossimo* of the above verbs is:

io ho	dormito	io mi sono	addormentato(a)
tu hai	servito	tu ti sei	servito(a)
egli ha	sentito	egli si è	sentito(a)
noi abbiamo		noi ci siamo	addormentati(e)
voi avete		voi vi siete	serviti(e)
essi hanno		essi si sono	sentiti(e)

EXERCISES

These exercises should be attempted after the corresponding Fluency Practice has been completely mastered.

Lessons I–III

(*a*) Answer the following questions both affirmatively and negatively:

È | il professore?
  | la cameriera?
  | un agente di polizia?
  | un buon albergo?
  | una camera grande?

(*b*) Answer affirmatively and negatively:

1. È | comodo il letto?
   | troppo piccola la camera?
   | a destra la stanza da bagno?
2. Sono | grandi i cassettoni?
   | comode le poltrone?
   | italiane le signore?
   | americani i signori?

(*c*) Answer both affirmatively and negatively:

1. È | inglese lei?
   | italiano(a) lei?
   | americano(a) lei?
   | scozzese lei?
2. Parla | inglese?
   | italiano?
   | americano?
   | spagnolo?
3. Fuma? Sale? Lavora molto?
   Entra? Ascolta? Beve?

(*d*) Say in the negative:

1. Entri!
2. Io salgo.
3. Ascolta?
4. Parli italiano!
5. Essa è piccola.
6. È gentile Giovanni?
7. È l'insegnante.
8. Scriva!

(*e*) Say in Italian:

1. Come in.
2. Don't come in.
3. Aren't you coming up?
4. I am coming up.
5. Don't speak so fast.
6. You speak Italian, don't you?
7. A gentleman is coming in.
8. He is the teacher.
9. He is smoking.
10. It is a large bed.
11. It is very comfortable.
12. Where is the bathroom?
13. There, on the left.
14. These are the rooms.
15. They are small, aren't they?

Lesson IV

(*a*) Replace the nouns in italics by pronouns:

1. Egli mette *i vestiti* nel guardaroba.
2. Essa chiude *la porta*.
3. Egli apre *il libro*.
4. Chiude *la valigia* lei?
5. Prende *la borsa da viaggio* lei?
6. Porta su *i bagagli* il facchino?
7. Posi *questa valigia* davanti alla finestra.
8. Non prenda *questo baule*.
9. Non chiuda *questa valigia*.
10. Chiuda *la porta*.
11. Apra *la finestra*.
12. Non guardi *questi libri*.

(*b*) Answer both affirmatively and negatively:

1. Le piace il vino (la birra, questo colore, questo profumo)?
2. Le pi*a*cciono le arance (le banane, le sigarette inglesi)?
3. Prende l'ombrello (la val*i*gia, questi libri, i bagagli)?
4. La cameriera apre le finestre (la porta, i cassetti, il guardaroba, la borsa da vi*a*ggio)?

(*c*) Give thc negative of:

1. Metta queste s*e*die nel giardino.
2. Esse sono nell'autorimessa (*or* nel garage).
3. È nel guardaroba l'ombrello?
4. È dietro alla porta?

5. Prenda quel tassì.
6. Le prenda.
7. Apra il ba*u*le.
8. Chiuda le finestre.
9. È lei nel giardino?
10. Essi sono nell'arm*a*dio.
11. Questo colore mi piace.
12. Preferisce questa *c*amera?

(*d*) Say in Italian:

1. Do you smoke?
2. Don't you speak English?
3. Aren't you American?
4. Isn't he bringing up the luggage?
5. Have you no smaller rooms?
6. Here is my luggage.
7. Give it to me.
8. I don't like this room.
9. Put the suitcase on the table.
10. Give me the travelling bag.
11. Don't put it on the bed.

Lesson V

(*a*) Answer the following questions:

1. Di che colore è il suo libro (il mio ombrello, il suo fazzoletto, il cappello dell'insegnante, la cravatta di quel ragazzo)?
2. Di che colore sono i suoi guanti (i suoi fazzoletti)?
3. Di che colore sono le sue scarpe (le sue calze)?
4. Dov'è il suo libro (ombrello, cappello, sopr*a*bito)?
5. Dov'è la sua val*i*gia (cam*i*cia, cravatta)?
6. Dove sono i suoi fazzoletti (guanti, cappelli)?
7. Dove sono le sue cravatte (calze, scarpe)?
8. Ha lei il mio ombrello (i miei guanti, i suoi libri, le mie scarpe)?

(*b*) Answer both affirmatively and negatively:

1. Ho io il suo fazzoletto (i suoi guanti, i suoi libri, le sue scarpe)?
2. Ha lei il mio cappello (le mie cravatte, i miei occhiali, la mia val*i*gia)?
3. Suo fratello ha la sua val*i*gia (la mia cravatta, il suo sopr*a*bito, i miei guanti)?

(*c*) Replace the words in italics by pronouns:

1. Porti su *i bagagli.*
2. Io metto il *soprabito* sulla sedia.
3. Io prendo *i guanti.*
4. Essa porta *il cappello verde.*
5. Metta *le scarpe* nel guardaroba.

(*d*) Replace the words in italics by *il suo, la sua, i suoi, le sue, il loro, la loro, i loro* or *le loro.*

1. La c*a*mera *di mio fratello.*
2. La c*a*mera *di mia sorella.*
3. La c*a*mera *dei miei cugini.*
4. Le cravatte *di mio padre.*
5. L'ombrello *di mia madre.*
6. La casa *dei miei nonni.*
7. I vestiti *di mia zia.*
8. I figli *di mio zio.*
9. Le c*a*mere *dei miei fratelli.*

(*e*) Say in Italian:

1. My brown hat is in the wardrobe.
2. Where is your umbrella?
3. It is behind that chair.
4. Is his tie grey or green?
5. Is her hat blue or black?
6. Are these your gloves?
7. Where are my handkerchiefs?
8. Aren't they on the chest of drawers?
9. Look! Here they are.
10. Their shoes are in front of the door.

Lesson VI

(*a*) Answer both affirmatively and negatively:

1. Mangia lei del form*a*ggio (della carne, delle sardine)?
2. Ha del pane lei (della carne, dei biscotti, dell'acqua)?
3. Sua sorella ha del burro (dell'insalata, della verdura)?

(*b*) Answer the following questions:

Quanti cappelli (*a*biti, cravatte, fazzoletti, lire) ha?

(*c*) Read these numbers:

7, 11, 13, 14, 15, 16, 18, 23, 34, 45, 54, 29, 38, 49, 57.

(*d*) Say in Italian:

1. What time is lunch?
2. What is there for supper?
3. What is the time now?
4. Do you like coffee?
5. Do you take sugar?
6. How many lumps do you take?
7. Is there any milk?
8. Please bring sugar and milk.
9. Haven't they any rolls?
10. There is no butter on the table.

Lesson VII

(*a*) Answer both affirmatively and negatively:

D*a*nzano	i signori?
C*a*ntano	le signore?
Lav*o*rano	i ragazzi?
Gi*o*cano	i bambini?
S*a*lgono	le ragazze?

(*b*) Insert the missing endings:

1. Noi and— al c*i*nema questa sera.
2. I miei genitori mi mand— dei pacchi.
3. Essa lavor— fino alle cinque.
4. La birra non mi piac—.
5. Ven— con me!
6. Egli parl— bene l'italiano.
7. Esse non cant—.

(*c*) Answer both affirmatively and negatively:

1. Viene dal teatro lei?
2. Va al c*i*nema?
3. Ho io il suo libro?
4. Ha lei il mio cappello?
5. Ascolta?
6. È la val*i*gia di sua sorella?
7. Sono i guanti di suo fratello?

(*d*) Say in Italian:

1. Can you sing?
2. Do you play the violin?
3. Let us dance.
4. Where are you going?
5. I am going to the casino.
6. Where are you coming from?
7. I am coming from the hotel.
8. Aren't they playing?
9. What time does he come from the office?
10. She is not coming from the station.

(*e*) Che ora è (che ore sono)?

6.15	9.50	12.10	2.25
7.30	10.05	12.30	3.32
8.45	11.40	1.55	5.20

Lesson VIII

(*a*) Say in the future:

1. Fa colazione alle otto.
2. Non ho abbastanza z*u*cchero.
3. Esse m*a*ngiano della minestra.
4. Sono d'accordo.
5. Andiamo in It*a*lia.
6. Esse sono in Austr*a*lia.
7. Essi hanno fame.
8. Tu hai molti libri.

(*b*) Answer these questions:

1. M*a*ngia molta carne lei?
2. Beve della birra?
3. Beve vino sua sorella?
4. Prende il caffè lei dopo pranzo?
5. Prenderà dello z*u*cchero?
6. Andrà in It*a*lia lei quest'anno?
7. Dove sarà lei questa sera?
8. Verrà qui domani suo fratello?
9. Quando avrà le vacanze lei?
10. Ha sete?

(*c*) Say in Italian:

1. Will you take soup?
2. What fish will there be?
3. You don't eat enough vegetables.
4. Don't eat too much meat.
5. What will you drink?
6. Does Maria drink coffee?
7. I shall eat a mushroom omelette.
8. My wife will take some fruit.
9. Where will you go this year?
10. We shall be in Switzerland a fortnight from today.

LESSON IX

(*a*) Add one of the following adjectives to each of the nouns (making it feminine or plural where necessary):

buono, cattivo, bello, gi*o*vane, v*e*cchio, nuovo, bianco, nero, italiano, lungo.

1. idea	6. scarpe
2. statua	7. signora
3. castello	8. giornale
4. città	9. via
5. cavallo	10. abit*u*dine

(*b*) Say in Italian:

1. Is there a bus stop near here?
2. Which bus must I take to go to the station?
3. What street is this?
4. Do I have to get off here?
5. You cannot go there by bus.
6. Can I take the bus?
7. Is it very far from here?
8. There is a bus stop in front of the station.
9. It is near the museum.
10. You can cross the road now.

LESSON X

(*a*) Answer the questions on page 61 both affirmatively and negatively.

(*b*) Replace the nouns in italics by pronouns:

1. Perchè gu*a*rdano *quella signora?*
2. Lei comprerà *questi fiori?*
3. Io scrivo *al mio amico.*
4. Non parli *a questi bambini.*
5. Noi aspettiamo *l'autobus.*
6. Spedisce un regalo *a sua sorella.*
7. Essa offre il posto *a un vecchio signore.*
8. Lei darà la m*a*ncia (= *tip*) *alla cameriera?*

(*c*) Say in Italian:

1. What a beautiful picture!
2. Will you buy it?
3. Will he sell it?
4. We are sending her a postcard.
5. Don't you want to write to her?
6. I shall see her tonight.
7. Don't tell her anything.
8. Will you speak to him?
9. Here is the manager. Let's ask him.
10. I do not know how much money to give them.

Lesson XI

(*a*) Read the following dates:

2-5-1950	18-4-1916	12-4-1921	1-1-1960
6-8-1851	30-6-1927	28-2-1776	16-4-1930
21-3-1903	11-7-1957	15-9-1899	23-11-1975

(*b*) Answer the following questions:

1. Che giorno della settimana è?
2. Che giorno sarà domani?
3. Qual'è la data di oggi? (Quanti ne abbiamo?)
4. Lei è nato nel 1952?
5. Qual'è il primo mese dell'anno?
6. Lei fa della ginn*a*stica ogni mattina?
7. Che cosa farà lei domani sera?
8. Lei legge molti romanzi?
9. Verrà qui lei domani?
10. È dom*e*nica domani?

(*c*) Say in Italian:

1. He has already arrived.
2. Where are you?
3. What are you doing?
4. Where are they?
5. What are they doing?

6. What are they saying?
7. What time will the train leave?
8. Have they any rooms?
9. They haven't any.
10. Will you stay for supper with us?

Lesson XII

(*a*) Replace the nouns in italics by pronouns:

1. Prenda *il quaderno.*
2. Porti *la carne.*
3. Mostrino *il biglietto.*
4. Comperi *i fiammiferi.*
5. Dica *il suo nome a questo signore.*
6. Porti *questi fiori alla signorina Luciana.*
7. Non f*a*ccia vedere *questa lettera a sua moglie.*
8. Egli venderà *l'automobile al mio amico Francesco.*
9. Spedirò *questo pacco a mia madre.*
10. Daranno *dei regali ai loro bambini.*
11. Che cosa dirà lei *a sua sorella?*
12. Lei restituirà *i libri al suo insegnante?*

(*b*) Say the above sentences in the negative.

(*c*) Say the sentences under (*a*) in the negative, replacing all nouns by pronouns.

(*d*) Reply both affirmatively and negatively, replacing the nouns by pronouns:

1. Le do io | il mio cappello?
la mia cravatta?
le mie scarpe?
2. Lei mi dà | il suo ombrello?
il suo orol*o*gio?
i suo guanti?
3. Lei porterà questi fiori | a suo zio?
a mia zia?
alle sue cugine?

(*e*) Say in Italian:

1. Why don't you show them (the cards) to her?
2. He will sell it (the car) to us.
3. Are there any peaches?
4. No, there aren't any.
5. Bring it (the cup) to her.
6. Send them (the books) to him.
7. Give it (the book) back to her.
8. Will you not show them (the cards) to me?
9. Will you not give us any?
10. Open it (the door).
11. Don't shut them (the windows).
12. She lends it (the umbrella) to you.
13. Let us sell it (the car) to him.

LESSON XIII

(*a*) Answer the questions on page 78 both affirmatively and negatively.

(*b*) Answer the following questions:

1. Mi ha visto lei ieri?
2. Ha mangiato delle uova lei questa mattina?
3. Che cosa ha bevuto?
4. Ha fatto il bagno?
5. Ha scritto al suo amico?
6. Ha parlato in italiano prima della lezione?
7. Le ha scritto suo cugino?
8. Le ha prestato il libro mio fratello?
9. Mi ha visto ieri sera a teatro?
10. Che cosa ha fatto domenica scorsa?
11. Ha visto il Signor Biagi?
12. Hanno venduto la loro casa i suoi amici?
13. Ha letto il giornale?
14. Hanno dormito bene le sue sorelle?

(*c*) Repeat the following sentences in the *Passato Prossimo:*

1. Essa legge tutti i giornali.
2. Gi*o*cano a carte tutte le sere.
3. Noi beviamo del vino bianco.
4. Io prendo del caffè nero.
5. Dove mette la val*i*gia?
6. Dorme mio fratello?
7. Facciamo una passeggiata.
8. Non cap*i*scono?
9. Ho sete.

Lesson XIV

(*a*) Answer the questions on page 84 both affirmatively and negatively.

(*b*) Answer the following questions:

1. Lei va spesso a teatro?
2. C'è andato ieri sera?
3. Ci andrà domani?
4. A che ora è venuto qui lei?
5. È venuta con lei sua sorella?
6. A che ora è uscito lei questa mattina?
7. È stato a Roma?
8. È arrivato alla Stazione T*e*rmini?
9. Quanti giorni c'è rimasto?
10. Vorrebbe andare in It*a*lia la settimana pr*o*ssima?

(*c*) Say in Italian:

1. Don't go there.
2. I went there last month.
3. I stayed there three weeks.
4. I came back on August 15th.
5. We left on July 23rd.
6. Hasn't she come back yet?
7. At what time did the train arrive?
8. Where have you been?

9. I went to the cinema.
10. What did you see?
11. Have you had your dinner?
12. What did you eat?
13. I should like to see her.

(*d*) Say the *Imperfetto, Passato Prossimo*, *Futuro* and *Condizionale* of:

1. Egli lavora.
2. Noi usciamo.
3. Io sono d'accordo.
4. Viene lei?
5. Essi hanno fame.
6. Io gli scrivo.
7. Essa me lo dice.
8. Dove vanno loro?

LESSON XV

(*a*) Answer the following questions:

1. A che ora si sveglia lei?
2. Lei si alza prima di sua sorella?
3. A che ora si alza suo fratello?
4. Quante ore ha dormito lei?
5. Come si chiama lei?
6. Come si chiama sua madre?
7. È suo questo libro?
8. A che ora è uscito lei questa mattina?

(*b*) Say in Italian:

1. Wake up.
2. Don't get up yet.
3. Our friend is washing.
4. Your father is shaving.
5. Is she getting dressed?
6. What time does he go to bed?
7. I went out with them.
8. Don't leave without him.
9. Have a good timc.
10. Sleep well.

(*c*) Read the following numbers:

64	23	71	377
74	32	92	893
85	54	105	1567
95	45	216	3459

Lesson XVI

(*a*) Repeat the sentences in Exercise VIII (*a*), page 102, in the *Passato Prossimo*.

(*b*) Answer the questions on page 93 both affirmatively and negatively.

(*c*) Say in Italian:

1. What time did you get up?
2. Let us go for a walk in the park.
3. The open air will do you good.
4. It is never too late.
5. It is so cold.
6. I caught a cold.
7. I have a headache and a sore throat.
8. It is not a good idea.
9. What did you do last night?
10. We went to the theatre.
11. What did you see?
12. Did you have a good time?

(*d*) Answer the following questions:

1. Fa bel tempo oggi?
2. Ha fatto bello ieri?
3. Piove adesso?
4. Ha piovuto questa mattina?
5. Che tempo ha fatto ieri?
6. Fa freddo oggi?
7. Fa caldo in inverno?
8. Piove spesso in estate?
9. Nevica spesso in inverno?
10. Dove passa le sue vacanze?

(*e*) Give the *Passato Prossimo*, *Imperfetto*, *Futuro* and *Condizionale* corresponding to:

1. Egli entra.
2. Essa si mette il cappello.
3. Io mi addormento.
4. Ha male ai denti lei?
5. Essi partono.
6. Essa si veste.

INDEX

Numbers refer to pages; those in brackets refer to the relevant Fluency Practice or Explanations section.